GRILL COOKBOOK

For Beginners

The Definitive Manual To Master Barbecue.All The Tips And Tricks You Need To Become A Grill Boss At First Try | Healthy, Delicious, And Tasty Recipes Included.

Will Stone

Table of Contents

Anthelme Brillat-Savarin

❋

The discovery of a new

dish does more for the

happiness of the human

race than the discovery of

a star

Will Stone

INTRODUCTION

Everyone, anywhere these days, has a favorite grilling method, specialized grill, or cookbook. Still, the result is almost always the same: moist, smoky, tasty meat and vegetables grilled over an open flame. The act of lighting a grill brings us to our past, encourages us to appreciate the outdoors, and reconnects us with our inner cave dwellers. For the perfect backyard BBQ, you don't need any machine or high-end device; all you need is a basic barbecue, some meat, and a couple of techniques up your sleeve.

Grilling is a dry heat cooking technique that uses clear, radiant heat. It allows you to cook meat and vegetables in a short amount of time, which is ideal for every night of the week.

Cooking on a grill uses a phenomenon known as thermal radiation. The heat source may be above or below what's being grilled, but when it's above the food, it's generally referred to as "broiled." The majority of grills get their heat from below. It can be either gas or charcoal.

In the present-day world, whenever you go to a restaurant, grilled food tops on the menu. It's what everyone enjoys despite of variating culture, age, social class, etc.

In the present times, grilled food is considered the festive food that is prepared for the community. It is mostly cooked outside and is the focal point of the social functions.

Cooking grilled food in everyday life is not hard. It is an easy and fast way of cooking that helps to preserve the nutrients of the food. Any rookie chef can do it. All you need is the basic techniques and your favorite protein.

This book provides a brief introduction to grilling, and gives detailed recipes that you can try at home and become a host to BBQ backyard parties.

CHAPTER 01

CONCEPT OF GRILLING

CHAPTER 1 - CONCEPT OF GRILLING

Background

Grilling dates back to the caveman age, when one of our forefathers found that keeping meat directly on an open fire for a prolonged period cooked the food. Cave dwellers most certainly came across creatures that had died in forest fires. They discovered that the scavenged meat was more delicious and simpler to chew than the fresh meat. Anthropologists are unable to agree on when our forefathers learned to prepare and cook the food. Cooking may have started somewhere around 300,000 years ago, when the fire was discovered, according to current figures.

Gratitude to our increasing culinary interest and need to know about the foods our forefathers used to eat, the heritage of barbecue is becoming a little easier to research. There was so little information about the origins of barbecue twenty years earlier. Until recently, culinary historians have been hard at work delving into the origins of barbecue.

Barbecue's popularity in the United States has its origins in the Caribbean; it is believed to have started with the Caribbean Taino Indians, who used a structure constructed of green sticks to smoke or dry meat. In his travel story, The Barbecue Feast: or, the Three Pigs of Peckham, Broiled Under an Apple-Tree, Edward Ward recorded one of the earliest English tales of barbecue.

For many Americans, grilling is a source of honor. Barbecue competitions, which began in the 1980s, now attract audiences of hundreds and thousands of spectators. Each state has its own distinct barbecue style, which varies in everything from the meat used to the sauce, the side dishes, and even the kind of wood used to cook it over.

Barbecue, like so many other distinctly "American" foods and cuisine, can be traced back to colonial America in the 18th century, especially the colonies along the south-eastern seaboard.

Eastern Carolina-style pit barbecue is a direct successor of the first American barbecue, starting with the entire hog and culminating in a magnificent mess of pulled pork doused in vinegar sauce and eaten with coleslaw on the side on a hamburger bun for as much as 14 hours over coals.

While the pioneers moved west, cultural differences emerged, resulting in 4 distinct barbecue types today. Western, Eastern, and South Carolina-style Carolina barbecue differ mostly in the sauce.

Kansas City is located in the heart of BBQ nation. There's a little bit of all there, too—pork and beef, shoulders and ribs, and so on. The sauce is what ties it together.

Texas has often preferred steak. Usually, brisket, dry-rubbed and smoked over mesquite with a to-mato-based sauce served on the table, almost as an afterthought.

1.1   What is grilling?

Cooking food on a rack over a heat source, such as ceramic briquettes heated by gas fires or char-coal fire, is known as grilling. Direct heat easily sears the external part of the cooked product, resulting in distinct sturdy, roasted, and sometimes gently charred tastes, as well as a pleasant crust. When food is cooked over medium heat, it also produces a smokier flavor.

1.2 What is a grill?

A grill is a cooking device with a grate or an open rack as the cooking surface and a fire source beneath. The heat source may be open flame (charcoal or gas) or electric, depending on the form of the grill.

Since food is cooked straight on the grill's grate or rack, the best foods for grilling are poultry and meats, though firm pork, shrimp, and vegetables may also be cooked on the grill.

Grill marks from the rack or grate are one of the features of food cooked on the grill. This impact can be accomplished by utilizing a grill plate, which is a specially built device. Since a grill pan has elevated ridges that can produce grill marks, purists argue that cooking on a grill pan is not actually grilling.

TYPES
OF GRILLS

CHAPTER 2 - TYPES OF GRILLS

A variety of ways classify the world's thousands, if not dozens, of distinct grills. You may categorize them based on the type of fuel they use, such as wood-burning grills, gas grills, and charcoal grills. You may group them by areas of origin, such as South American grills or Southeast Asian grills. However, from the perspective of a griller, the most functional method is to arrange the fire and position the food for frying. It is what decides the temperature at which the food can grill and how easily it can cook. Understanding and monitoring these factors can determine how effective you are as a grill master..

2.1   Vessel Grill

The term coined to define thick-walled, deep ceramic grills that cook food using both radiant heats from the sidewalls and direct warmth from the coals. Instead of using a grill grate, food is often grilled directly on the walls or on a perpendicular spit located within the firebox.

Iran's tandoor, India's tandoor, and kamado cookers are all examples.

Roasting at high temperatures, smoking and grilling are all possible with the kamado cooker.

Flatbreads, such as Indian naan that are cooked directly on the tandoor's walls, are best suited for these types of grills. On a vertical spit, kebabs, ham, fish steaks, tiny lamb and goat wings, peppers, and paneer cheese are all grilled.

2.2   Smoker Grill

While smoking is one of the oldest ways of cooking and storing foods, the smoker as a mobile back-yard barbecue grill is a twentieth-century North American innovation. Grilling is practiced all around the world, but not all grill societies burn.

Included are Texas offset barrel smokers, box smokers from North America, China, and Europe, upright water smokers, and pellet/sawdust smokers from North America (such as the Traeger and Bradley).

Smoking, indirect grilling of wood smoke at low to moderate temperatures foodstuffs, are ideally suited for these grills.

It is adequate to cook foods like the rough, tasty cuts of beef like ribs and brisket.

2.3   Rotisserie Grill

This grill brings movement to the often-stagnant grilling method. A turnspit's steady, gentle rotating level out the cooking period, baste the meat, melt fat, and brown the outside. Foods that are spit-roasted come out fresh on the exterior and juicy on the inside.

Included under this category are Tuscany's and Germany's wood rotisseries, France's gas wall rotisseries, Malaysia's and Singapore's charcoal chicken wing rotisseries, and the infrared ones incorporated into American gas grills. Grill masters use vertical rotisseries to render Turkish doner, Greek gyro, and Middle Eastern shawarma in the eastern Mediterranean and the Middle East.

Ideally used for combining the benefits of both indirect and direct grilling. The food directly faces the heat, much as in the direct grilling, except in indirect grilling, the food is cooked adjoining, rather than directly above the flames.

Cylindrical and fatty ingredients, such as entire poultry, chicken wings, pigs, whole hogs, and rib roasts, work best with this grill

2.4 Open Pit and Campfire Grills

Grilling (or cooking) used to be performed over or adjoining to a campfire rather than on a grill. This ancient method is still widely used, particularly in America.

Included under this category are Argentina's Asado and Brazil's Fogo de Cho—meats grilled in front of a fire—typify open-pit grilling. The Pacific Northwest's salmon "bakes," Connecticut's planked shad, and roasting marshmallows on sticks to produce s'mores are all examples of campfire grilling. Radiant-heat roasting is what it's used for.

Whole calf, pig, goat, and tuna, skin-on salmon fillets, and beef ribs are the best choices to be cooked on these types of grills.

2.5   Open Grills

The most basic of all grills is a stone or metal box with a wood, charcoal, or propane fire at the bottom and food directly over the fire. The grill grate is not needed.

Table grills from North America and Europe, South American parrillas, the Balkan mangal, the Italian fogolar, Indonesian saté grills, Asian bucket grills, and the Australian flattop grill are only a few examples.

It is ideally used for direct grilling on high heat.

Kebabs, Satés, steaks, cuts, fish fillets, veggies, and other tiny, fresh, speedily foods are perfect for cooking using these grills.

2.6 Closed Grills

When you combine an open grill with a tall lid that you can lift and drop, you have a covered grill. This could seem to be a minor advancement, but the closed grill allows you to incorporate two more essential live-fire cooking techniques into your oeuvre: indirect grilling and smoking.

The gas grill, kettle grill, and 55-gallon steel-drum grill are all included under this category.

Larger or thicker items may be directly grilled on this grill. Grilling and vaping done in an indirect manner are ideally suited for this.

Foods that go well with this type of grilling include beef and fish steaks, as well Meats with higher fat content, such as double-thick veal, pork chops, pork back ribs, pork shoulder, and also entire duck and chicken.

BASIC GRILLING TIPS

CHAPTER 3 - BASIC GRILLING TIPS

3.1 Preheat the Grill

To bring the best out of your cooking, grills, just like the ovens, they should always be preheated. Preheat the grill for around 15 minutes with the cover closed.

The average temperature under the cover can exceed 500°F with all of the coals glowing red or all of the gas burners on high. The warmth loosens any bits of food that have clung to the grate, rendering it simple to wipe them down.

Preheating the grill prevents food from binding to the grate and ensures that the grate is hot enough to sear adequately.

3.2 Put the Lid on the Grill

The lids aren't only there to cover the grills; selectively utilizing them can aid in the production of smoky flavors. Not only can it hold the grates hot enough to sear the food, but it also makes the food warm.

It reduces cooking time while still preventing food from drying out. By reducing oxygen, it avoids flare-ups.

3.3 Keep the Grill Clean

When food splatters on your cooking grate, and it's wet, use a stainless-steel brush to clean it. This measure isn't all for the sake of hygiene. It also keeps the food from sticking to the pan. If there are some loose bristles on the cooking grates or brush, it is suggested to replace them.

3.4 Make Sure You're Cooking on a Clean Table

To achieve some sort of healthy grilling (or cooking, for that matter) start with a clean slate. Clean the grates with a wire brush to clear any food debris or char. Then, using paper towels or a rag, rub them off with vegetable oil. Some broken-off brush bristles can be scooped up as well.

3.5 Create Distinct Grilling "Zones"

When dealing with a grill, especially one with a wide surface area on which you could be cooking several products, it's a good idea to create separate "zones," especially if you're cooking several things on your grill. By holding one part of the oven at a lower temperature, you may build cooking zones. You should switch your meat and vegetables to a cooler location when they begin to cook through to slow down the operation.

3.6 Priority Should Be Given to Safety

Still, read the reference manuals if you're confused about how to handle the tools. Often, use separate utensils with different kinds of proteins to prevent cross-contamination.

3.7 Choose the Right Meat

Choosing the correct protein-packed meats is one of the most critical moves before you even start grilling. Meats that are perfect for fast grilling can yield and not sprout up when touched. Good grilling options have meats that suit this definition that have a little marbling. It's important to remember that lean meats are more likely to overcook and dry out.

3.8 Grass-Fed Beef Is the Way to Go

We're all about saving money and keeping a close eye on our pockets, but it's worth it to splurge on high-quality meat whenever possible. Meat raised without hormones or antibiotics and handled humanely would still taste better than the Soylent Green industrial meat served in most restaurants. Spend time doing your research to guarantee you're getting the finest meat possible.

3.9 Get to Know Those Lesser-Known Cuts

Beef tenderloin, sirloin steak, and rib-eye steaks are all common choices, but they're far from the only ones. There are many lean cuts on a cow that you might not be familiar with, and if prepared properly, they can be exceptionally tender and tasty.

The petite tender, also known as the teres major, is one of Heitzeberg's favorites. The petite tender is a lesser-known shoulder muscle that is flavorful, lean, and tender, just slightly less than tenderloin. It's better if you grill it rapidly over a high heat source.

3.10 Use the Smoker to Your Benefit

Since they're built with various parts and are ideal for slower roasted foods like brisket and chicken, charcoal grills with smokers are perfect for cooking various dishes over long periods of time. Before making your food cook for hours, you have to make sure your smoker has adequate water and humidity. Under these circumstances, brined and curing goods perform well. Wrapping slow-roasted vegetables in foil often give corn and sweet potatoes a fantastic confit effect.

3.11 For the Best Char, Use Gas Grills

Gas grills are safer than charcoal grills if you want a burnt smell. Gas grills can generate more heat, allowing for better sear and char taste. If you're using a barbecue grill, though, you can avoid over-greasing the coals to reduce flames and burning.

3.12 Make the Grill Automatically Non-Stick

Sometimes people use oil to lubricate their grills so that food doesn't stick. However, there is a simpler way to make a non-stick surface. To stop wasting a lot of oils, cut a potato in half and rub it on the hot grates. The grill would automatically become non-stick as a result of this.

3.13 Allow Time for the Meat to Rest Before Grilling

If you're planning to barbecue some steak, don't pull it out of the fridge just before you start cooking it. Allow the steak to rest for at least 30 minutes before cooking it. Larger, thicker cuts, such as a porterhouse or a bone-in rib-eye, need this. When you put a frozen steak on the grill, it will not cook uniformly and will dry out quickly.

3.14 Cook Evenly While Using Your Palm

Grilling utensils can assist you in flipping your meat and vegetables for even frying, but often what you need is your thumb. Create a thumbprint indentation in each patty before placing it on the grill to ensure even cooking. When the patty shrinks throughout the cooking period, the indentation allows it to keep its form rather than expanding.

3.15 Invest in a Good Pair of Tongs

To place food on the grill and pass it about when it's frying, it's a smart idea to invest in a good pair of tongs. Tongs with a long handle and a spring-loaded mechanism serve as an additional set of paws.

3.16 Maintain a Low and Gradual Rate of Heat

When people barbecue, they often make the error of getting the grill overly hot and attempting to cook at extremely high temperatures. Instead, it is suggested that you take it slow and simple. Learn how your grill's vents operate so you can properly regulate the temperature. To produce various taste profiles, look at reverse searing and other slow cooking techniques.

3.17 Purchase a Good Thermometer

Since heat increases, thermometers are usually fixed on the grill lid, so this ensures they will register 50° colder than if they were mounted on the grill itself. When it comes to grilling, an instant-read thermometer is your best buddy. Test the internal temperature of your meat with it.

3.18 Don't Juggle the Food Too Much

Although it might be tempting to pass the food across the grill while it heats, this is not recommended. Avoid throwing the food around so far on the barbecue. Allow it to stay on the grate for as long as possible to ensure even cooking and good grill marks.

3.19 Try Your Hand at the Robatayaki Process

Try the Robatayaki system if you want to please your visitors. The Robatayaki (or Robata) grilling process is a common Japanese technique for slowly grilling skewered meats, vegetables, and fish over charcoal. Slow grilling is an excellent way to develop flavor layers in basic meat and vegetable dishes.

3.20 Finish With a Drizzle of BBQ Sauce

It is recommended that the BBQ sauce not be applied to the chicken before it has reached a certain temperature. The sauce can only be cooked on the grill for a few minutes. It can flame if left on the grill for too long.

3.21 To Infuse Spice into Your Beef, Dip It in a Sauce

You could be dunking while you're marinating your beef. Thin out your preferred marinade with water to achieve a flavor comparable to soy sauce. Cook the meat on the grill after dipping it in it.

Take the meat off the grill a few minutes and dip it into the marinade. Then quickly return it to the barbecue. This approach would not only lower the calorie count of your marinade, but will also enhance the flavor of your beef. Since the marinade is applied to the meat in thin coats, you get optimum flavor without using the full amount of sugar.

3.22 Prepare a Dry Rub Ahead of Time

Dry rubs are a perfect way to give a lot of spice to your meats without consuming a lot of calories and fat. So, if you're going to barbecue ahead of time, use a dry rub instead of sauces and marinades.

Using salt to your dry rub is a simple way to improve the taste of your beef. This will cause the rub to reach the meat and season it all the way through. You must rub your meats 12 to 24 hours ahead of time for a rub to be effective.

3.23 Cook for the Sake of Appearance

There's nothing like getting those new grill marks on a juicy cut of beef. The beef should be positioned at a 45-degree angle to the grill grate to achieve this. To make a crosshatch pattern, sear the meat at a 45-degree angle, then rotate it 90 degrees and sear it once more.

3.24 On the Barbecue, Undercook the Fish

When the fish is removed from the grill, the remaining heat is sufficient to cook it. Remove the salmon from the pan only before it reaches medium-rare. It should be a fine platform by the time it's able to work.

3.25 After Grilling, Enable the Meat to Rest

It's tempting to cut through the steak right after it comes off the grill, but it's important to let it sit for a couple of minutes. Many people break through a delicious slice of meat without making it hang or recover after grilling it. Allowing the meat to stand for about 4 minutes before cutting it allows you to enjoy the consistency.

EALTHY
GRILLING TIPS

CHAPTER 4 - EALTHY GRILLING TIPS

All and all, preferring "grilled" foods over "cooked" foods is one of the cardinal laws of eating well at restaurants. Since there's no batter covering or dripping fat on grilled food, it's a better alternative.

After all, there's something about grilling that makes food appear and taste amazing. Is it the smoky flavor, the pleasant marinade flavors, the grill lines that shape on the beef, or the fresh taste that comes from cooking something rapidly over high heat?

However, grilling also has some of the dietary disadvantages that are explained in the next chapter. But fear not grilling enthusiasts: there is a fresh, safe way to grill! If you follow these guidelines, you will be able to grill guilt-free.

4.1   Fruits and Vegetables on the Grill

Grilling fruits and vegetables, whether or not you're grilling meat or seafood to go with them, is a brilliant idea. We all need more fruits and vegetables in our diets, and this is a delicious way to do so. I'm sure I don't have to tell you that consuming fruits and vegetables is good for you in a variety of respects, like lowering the risk of coronary heart attack, stroke, obesity, and some forms of cancer.

But the best part has yet to come: Grilled fruits and vegetables do not produce PAHs or HCAs. Plus, if you're consuming grilled beef, using antioxidant-rich fruits and vegetables with your meal is a fantastic idea.

Grill-friendly fruits and vegetables include:

1. Tomatoes

2. Bell peppers

3. Eggplant

4. Onions

5. Zucchini

6. Endive

7. Mango

8. Pear

9. Pineapple

10. Apple

4.2 Grill Wisely, Grill Lightly

When grilling beef, begin with lean cuts that have been stripped of clear fat and skin to reduce the volume of fat that drips onto the coals. You're off to a healthy start whether you barbecue a really lean cut of beef or pork or skinless chicken..

4.3 Reduce the amount of time you waste grilling

Smaller pieces of beef, seafood, and fish can be grilled to ensure that they heat quickly and waste less time on the grill. Another technique is to cook the beef, seafood, and poultry first in the oven or microwave, then finish on the barbecue.

4.4 Keep Flipping

According to recent studies using hamburger patties, tossing food regularly can help prevent the development of HCAs. Using tongs or spatulas instead of a fork to transform meat without piercing it, produces juices that drip onto the coals.

4.5 Use Skewers

Threading tiny pieces of meat or fish on a skewer is a fun way to reduce back on grilling time. Scallops and shrimp are also great options for skewers. It's highly advised to mix in bell pepper and onion slices, zucchini slices, cherry tomatoes, and tiny mushrooms with bits of beef, chicken, or seafood.

But what if you don't have any skewers? It's no concern. As skewers, you can use rosemary branches. They infuse a touch of rosemary into the food as it heats, and it allows for a spectacular show.

4.6 Marinate well

The thought of infusing spice into foods, fruits, and vegetables by soaking them in a delicious marinade has to appeal to you. Wines, vinegar, lemon or lime juice, low-sodium soy sauce, sugar, garlic, onions, herbs, and spices are all common marinade ingredients. To reduce the volume of fat that drips onto the coals, use low-fat or fat-free marinades on your grilled meats, seafood, and poultry.

Keep the following marinating suggestions in mind::

1. Look for items or recipes that use olive or canola oil while purchasing canned marinades or producing your own (and that only use a little oil).

2. Any items that have been marinating for more than 1/2 hour should be refrigerated.

3. Don't waste the meal with the oil that the meat was marinating in before grilling. Set aside some of your marinades before adding the meat for this reason.

4. Meats and poultry can marinate for at least 1 to 2 hours, while fish and vegetables just require an hour

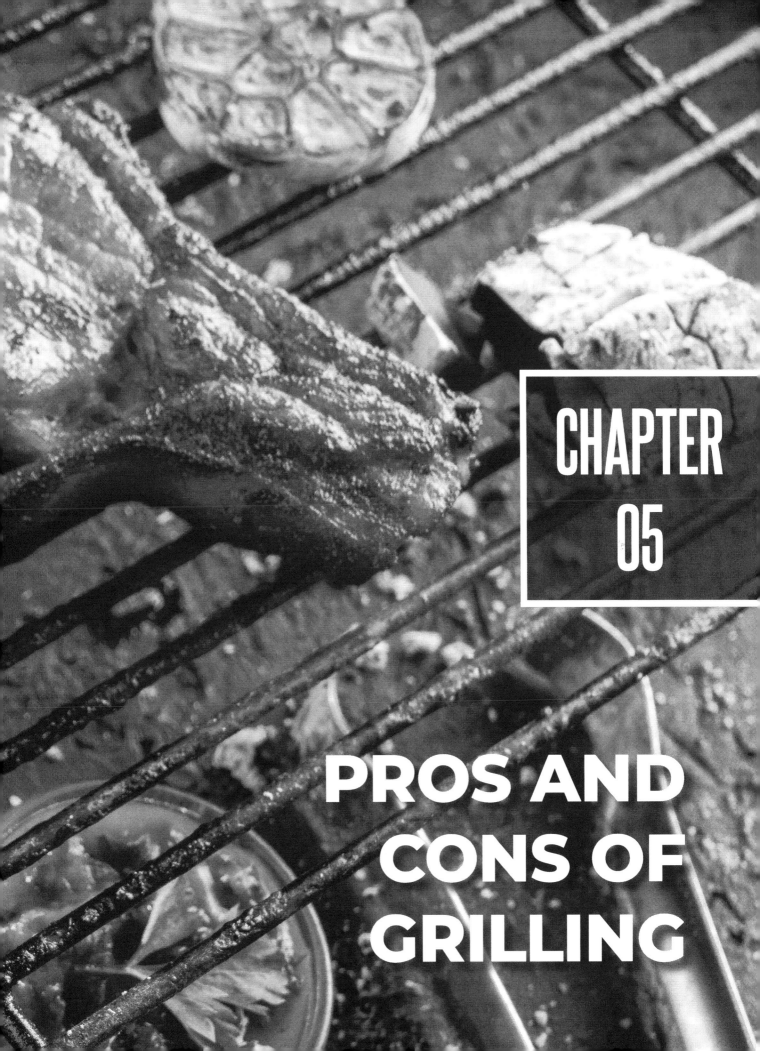

CHAPTER
05

PROS AND
CONS OF
GRILLING

CHAPTER 5 - PROS AND CONS OF GRILLING

5.1 Benefits of Grilling

When opposed to food cooked in the oven or on the burner, grilling has health benefits. Consider the following five health advantages. We'll even offer you several pointers on how to cook safe, balanced meals.

5.2 Grilled foods have less amount of fat

Food that is grilled should not have any extra fat. When you're grilling, the fat drips off the grates. Consider burgers cooked in a frying pan. Even as you move the meat to your dish, the fat pools on the skillet. Furthermore, the fat is made on the barbecue.

5.3 Grilled food preserves the nutrients

Meat that has been grilled retains more nutrients, including thiamine and riboflavin. These nutrients are essential for good health. It also has nutrients that are similar to those found in beef.

5.4 Grilled food is healthy

Did you realize that when vegetables are cooked, they preserve their nutrients and vitamins? This is especially true for vegetables that have low water content. Grilled vegetables are often always tossed and seasoned young. Cooking vegetables in either grilled way, whether wrapped in tin foil or just grilled bare, has further nutritious benefits.its.

5.5   Grilling is a social exercise and takes you outside

Grilling takes you and your guests outside. Although grilling, several households engage in other sports. Grilling allows you to spend some time outside. Outdoor physical workouts, in comparison to your meals, are a good addition to your diet

5.6   The use of butter is to be avoided in grilling

Grilling no longer necessitates the use of butter! All of the juices from the meats and vegetables ooze out, making it taste better. This often entails consuming fewer calories. Furthermore, it reduces the number of harmful substances in your bloodstream

Criticism of Grilling

5.7   From the standpoint of exercise

Grilling, as previously said, necessitates a few basic skills. It's important to understand a few fundamental explanations behind the apparatus you're working with. What is the reason for this? Since it's simple to overcook food when grilling. We will agree that charred or properly burned beef tastes fantastic and has fewer calories, but it is terrible for your health. Maybe not at all. Besides, we all know that grills just operate at really high temperatures. When the intense heat of the grill meets the proteins in the meat, a large number of potential carcinogens such as polycyclic aromatic hydrocarbons (PAHs) and heterocyclic amines (HCAs) are formed in the beef.

The extra fat and sauce that melts from the product on the grates and in the china vaporizes and compresses in the food often contributes to the distinctive pungent taste. Were you conscious, though, that this divinely delicious char is slightly harmful? What is the reason for this? As a consequence of the formation of advanced glycation end products, which may lead to diabetes, cardiac disease, and Alzheimer's disease, among other things. Undercooked meat is more harmful than overcooked meat. There are a few instances where you buy just the perfect crispy exterior, yet the meat is raw. These foods are very harmful to a person's health.

5.8   From the standpoint of grilling

Even though oil grills have numerous advantages over conventional charcoal grills, citizens choose to use the latter despite their numerous advantages. To begin, grilling (outdoor) may be done at any time during the summer. If you choose to barbecue in the winter, indoor grilling may be frantic and cluttered because it can blacken the roof and walls. Furthermore, someone assigned the task of grilling will be unwilling to enjoy something else because the job necessitates a great deal of constant attention.

To stop burning or charring, we will normally have to move the meat. To get started experimenting with a charcoal barbecue, you'll need a lot of planning and time. You must burn the charcoal until it is almost white. Furthermore, the smoke can get into the lungs as well as the food, making it toxic. After the grilling is over, the cleaning may be very exhausting. Charcoal produces a lot of smoke, while gas grills do not. Soot can form in your beef as a result of insufficient oxygen delivery.

Furthermore, you will want premium-grade beef for cooking solely to ensure that your quality of life is not jeopardized. It is, once again, an additional expense since this form of meat is very costly. As an example, consider purchasing premium-quality beef and then trimming it out by mistake. Yes, this is just what happens to the majority of people, with the exception of some who are skilled during the season. Grilling is prohibited in certain apartments because it increases the chances of the other catching fire. Nonetheless, there have been many instances in which a small blaze started by a barbecue forced the evacuation of the whole building's inhabitants.

Furthermore, broiled foods cannot be re-heated effectively and must be consumed immediately. Of necessity, if a large quantity of food is cooked on the grill at the same time, the taste would be uniform. The beef will not tenderize, and it will be difficult and time-consuming to prepare. As a result, your concern is: what is the aim of deciding on different issues? Why do people like to barbecue if there are too many dangers? There will be certain items that will kill it all.

Watch the food or you would easily get burnt; the meat could be raw or overcooked; the smoke would irritate the eyes

5.9   From an ecological standpoint

Grilling on a charcoal grill is also a popular option, and even though it provides us with delicious food, it is very harmful to the environment. Almost everybody is aware that the burning of charcoal produces further soot and smoke, which pervades the environment and can have an effect on our circulatory system and eyes. Nobody likes seeing smoke in their eyes.

5.10 From using a low-cost perspective

Now, one of the most common types of grills is the oil grill. When opposed to common grills, they are easier to clean during consumption. The former, on the other hand, is very costly. A good fuel grill will set you back about 300 $. As a result, even though it meets the difference in the stomach, it will create a massive one in the pocket.

Infrared burners are similar to oil grills. They were selected because they have clear heat, allowing the meat to be prepared quickly on the grill. However, there is a disadvantage: infrared grills are expensive and, due to their slim design, can be difficult to transport. Furthermore, the handheld ones are unsuitable for daily use and small gatherings. Furthermore, they do not need a low-temperature control alternative. As a result, they might not be suitable for leafy fish and vegetables.

CHAPTER 06

VEGETABLES AND SIDES RECIPES

CHAPTER 6 - VEGETABLES AND SIDES RECIPES

6.1   CHILI-RUBBED JICAMA STEAKS WITH QUESO FRESCO

Ready in about: 20 minutes - Servings: 2 - Difficulty: easy

Ingredients:

- 1 tsp. of chili powder.

- 1 lb. jicama, peeled and cut into half-inch-thick slices.

- Lime wedges for serving.

- 1 tbsp. of neutral oil, like grapeseed or corn.

- Salt and black pepper.

- 4 oz. of crumbled queso fresco cheese.

Instructions:

1. Preheat a charcoal or gas grill to medium-high heat and place the rack about 4 inches from the blaze. In a big mixing bowl, combine the oil, chili powder, and a pinch of salt and pepper. Toss in the jicama until uniformly covered.

2. Place the jicama on the grill and cook for 2 minutes, or until golden brown. Allow to grill for another 2 to 3 minutes after turning the slices and adding the queso fresco. With lime wedges, serve hot or at room temperature.

6.2   TERIYAKI CABBAGE STEAKS

Ready in about: 1 hour - Servings: 6 - Difficulty: hard

Ingredients:

- ½ cup of mirin—or ¼ cup of honey mixed with ¼ cup of water.

- 1 tsp. of minced garlic.

- 1 small cabbage cored and cut crosswise into one and a half-inch-thick slices.

- Half cup of soy sauce.

- 1 tbsp. of minced fresh ginger.

- 2 tbsp. of chopped scallions.

- 2 tbsp. of neutral oil, like grapeseed or corn.

- Lemon wedges for serving.

- Salt and black pepper.

Instructions:

1. Heat a charcoal or gas grill to a medium-high temperature, leaving a section of the grill cool for indirect grilling, and place the rack about 4-inches from the blaze. In a shallow saucepan over medium-low heat, mix the soy sauce and mirin and simmer for 2 to 3 minutes, or until the mixture starts to bubble. Take the pan off the heat and stir in the garlic, ginger, and scallions.

2. Oil the cabbage slices and season with pepper and salt. Close the grill cover and position the cabbage on the cool side of the grill. Cook for 40 to 45 minutes, testing and turning regularly until leaves are quickly pierced with a sharp knife. Brush the cabbage liberally with the teriyaki mixture and transfer it to the cooler portion of the grill until it is soft. Cook for 3 to 5 minutes, rotating once or twice and brushing with more of the sauce until it's browned.

3. Serve the cabbage hot or warm with lemon wedges and any leftover teriyaki sauce.

6.3   VIETNAMESE-STYLE PORTOBELLO MUSHROOMS

Ready in about: 20 minutes - Servings: 4 - Difficulty: easy

Ingredients:

- ¼ cup of fresh lime juice.

- 1 fresh seeded and minced hot red chili.

- ½ tsp. of sugar.

- 4 large portobello mushrooms, stem removed.

- ¼ cup of peanut oil.

- 2 tbsp. of chopped fresh mint, plus more for garnish.

- 1 tbsp. of fish sauce.

- Salt and lots of black pepper as per your taste.

Instructions:

1. 1Heat a gas charcoal grill to high heat, then place the rack 4 inches from the blaze. Combine the oil, juice, mint, chili, sugar, and fish sauce in a mixing bowl and season to taste with pepper and salt. Around half of this mixture can be rubbed all over the mushrooms.

2. Grill the mushrooms with the tops of their caps facing away from the blaze for 5 to 8 minutes or before they tend to tan. Turn and brush with the remaining marinade. 5 to 10 minutes more on the grill before tender and well browned all over. Serve hot, warm, or at room temperature, garnished with more mint.

6.4   CHARRED PEPPERS

Ready in about: 1 hour and 20 minutes - Servings: 6 - Difficulty: hard

Ingredients:

- 2 or so tbsp. of olive oil.
- Fresh lemon juice, capers, or anchovies (optional)
- 12 or more long peppers, red, green or both.
- Salt (optional)

Instructions:

1. Make a roaring fire. Wood is best, but charcoal is a close second. There can be no more than 3 or 4 inches between the rack and the fire, and peppers should be added only when the flames begin to die down; there would be no flare-up.

2. Place peppers on the grill in a single layer to avoid overcrowding. Turn them as they blacken to ensure that they char on all or almost all surfaces. Move them to a bowl where you can pile them up when they end.

3. Allow cooling. Peel and seed the peppers, rinsing the residual seeds and skin with as little water as practicable. But don't go overboard: a few seeds and scraps of skin would suffice. Often, the closest the peppers are to being entire, the more appealing they are.

4. Serve with a drizzle of olive oil and a touch of salt, if necessary. Capers and anchovies, as well as lemon juice, aren't likely to harm. These would hold for at least a week in the refrigerator.

6.5   POTATO FONDANTES WITH OREGANO

Ready in about: 40 minutes - Servings: 6 - Difficulty: moderate

Ingredients:

- 1 ½ tbsp. of unsalted butter.
- 3 lb. of medium potatoes.
- 2 tbsp. of canola oil.
- ½ tsp. of salt.
- 3 tbsp. of coarsely chopped fresh oregano.

Instructions

1. Remove some eyes and dark marks; just don't peel the potatoes. In a wide (ideally 10-inch) non-stick skillet, split potatoes in half lengthwise and place cut side down in 1 sheet.

2. Transfer 1 ½ cups water, oil, butter, oregano, and salt to the pot. Get the mixture to a boil over high pressure, then switch off the heat. Reduce the heat to medium and continue to cook for another 20 to 25 minutes. By this time, the water should have evaporated, and the potatoes should be well browned in butter and oil.

3. Flip the potatoes over and brown them gently on the other side for 2 or 3 minutes.

6.6   GRILLED MUSHROOM ANTIPASTO SALAD

Ready in about: 40 minutes - Servings: 4 to 6 - Difficulty: moderate

Ingredients:

- 7 tbsp. of extra-virgin olive oil, divided.
- 2 tbsp. of Champagne vinegar or white wine vinegar.
- 1 tsp. of dried oregano.
- 2 oz. Parmesan shaved.
- ¼ cup of drained Peppadew peppers in brine, coarsely chopped.
- 2 lb. assorted mushrooms, wiped clean, trimmed, torn into big pieces if large.
- Kosher salt.
- 1 tsp. of Aleppo-style pepper.
- 1 garlic clove, finely grated.
- ½ cup of Castelvetrano olives, coarsely chopped.

Instructions:

1. 1Heat a grill to extreme temperatures. In a wide mixing bowl, toss the mushrooms with 3 tbsp. of oil. Let it grill for 2 to 6 minutes, rotating periodically with tongs until slightly charred. Season it with salt and return to the cup.

2. In a shallow bowl, whisk together the Aleppo-style pepper, vinegar, garlic, oregano, and the remaining 4 tbsp. of oil; season with black pepper and salt. Toss the mushrooms in the sauce to seal them. Toss in the olives, Parmesan, and Peppadew peppers once well combined. Then serve after combining everything.

6.7 GRILLED POTATO SALAD WITH CHILES AND BASIL

Ready in about: 40 minutes - Servings: 4 - Difficulty: moderate

Ingredients:

- ½ cup of kosher salt, plus more.

- 3 tbsp. of fish sauce.

- ¼ cup plus 3 tbsp. of extra-virgin olive oil, plus more for drizzling.

- 1 large red onion.

- 2 cups of basil leaves.

- 2 lb. baby Yukon Gold potatoes.

- ⅔ cup of unseasoned rice vinegar.

- 1 tbsp. of honey.

- 2 red Fresno chilies, thinly sliced.

- 3 garlic cloves.

- 2 tbsp. of toasted sesame seeds.

Instructions:

1. In a big saucepan, cover potatoes with 3 quarts of water. With half cup of salt, stir it in over medium-high pressure, bring to a boil. Reduce heat to medium-low and proceed to cook for another 12 minutes or until potatoes are only soft when stabbed with a skewer or paring knife. Drain and set aside to cool.

2. Meanwhile, preheat the grill to medium. In a shallow bowl, combine the vinegar, honey, fish sauce, and 3 tbsp. of oil. Add the chilies and mix well. Put aside the dressing after seasoning it with salt.

3. Break the onion in half through the base, then cut half into 5 wedges, keeping the root in place.

4. In a broad mixing cup, finely grind the garlic. With ¼ cup of oil whisked in Toss, the onion wedges into the mixing bowl. When you add the potatoes to the dish, softly smash them with your hands and toss gently to cover them in garlic oil. Season with salt and pepper.

5. Put for 12 to 15 minutes on the fire, rotating periodically, before potatoes and onion wedges are charred all over. When the onions and the potatoes are done grilling, clean out the bowl you used to throw them in, then add them to it.

6. Toss the potatoes in the dressing to cover them. Add basil and sesame seeds, tearing some large leaves in half. Taste and adjust the seasoning with salt if necessary, then mix to blend.

7. In a serving dish, position the potato salad. Drizzle some oil on top.

6.8 GRILLED-SCALLION SALAD

Ready in about: 25 minutes - Servings: 4 to 6 - Difficulty: easy

Ingredients:

- 1 tbsp. of sesame oil.
- 2 tbsp. of gochugaru or 1 tbsp. of chili flakes.
- 2 tsp. of sugar.
- 1 lb. of scallions left untrimmed.
- ⅓ cup rice vinegar.
- 1 tbsp. of sesame seeds.

Instructions:

1. Brush the scallions with sesame oil and grill over medium-high flame, rotating once, for 5 to 10 minutes, or until charred and soft.

2. Toss with gochugaru, vinegar, sesame seeds, and sugar in a large mixing bowl. Serve right away.

6.9 TOMATO BRUSCHETTA

Ready in about: 10 minutes - Servings: 4 to 6 - Difficulty: easy

Ingredients:

- 2 garlic cloves, 1 grated, 1 halved.
- ¼ tsp. sea salt.
- Extra-virgin olive oil for drizzling.
- Fresh basil.
- 4 small finely chopped tomatoes.
- ½ tsp. of red wine vinegar or balsamic vinegar.
- Freshly ground black pepper.
- 6 to 8 slices of rustic country bread.

Optional:

- 2 tbsp. of capers.
- 6 Kalamata olives, finely chopped.

Instructions:

1. Combine the tomatoes, vinegar, grated garlic, salt, and a few grinds of pepper in a medium mixing bowl. Whisk in the olives and capers before using.

2. Drizzle the bread slices with olive oil and barbecue or toast until finely charred. Dust garlic on the hot bread with the split side of the garlic halves. Add the tomato mixture and new basil on top.

6.10 BARBECUED EGGPLANT AND PINE NUT APPETIZER

Ready in about: 30 minutes - Servings: 8 - Difficulty: easy

Ingredients:

- 2 tomatoes.
- 1 ½ tsp. of salt.
- 2 finely chopped garlic cloves.
- ¼ cup of pine nuts.
- 3 tbsp. of chopped fresh parsley.
- 2 medium eggplants.

- ⅓ cup fresh lemon juice.
- Freshly ground black pepper to taste.
- ½ cup olive oil.
- ¼ cup of finely chopped scallions, including the green part.
- Small squares of pumpernickel or flatbread.

Instructions:

1. Using a fork, poke eggplants all over and put over hot coals on a barbecue grill, rotating periodically until all sides are scorched. Turning the eggplants is simpler with a skewer threaded into each one.

2. Cover eggplants in foil and roast until tender over coals. Cook tomatoes over coals with a skewer or fork before the skins wrinkle.

3. Place the eggplants and tomatoes in a bowl after peeling them. Using a fork or a potato masher to mash the potatoes.

4. Combine the lemon juice, pepper, salt, garlic, pine nuts, and oil in a mixing plastic cup. Serve with pumpernickel squares or flatbread, garnished with scallions and parsley.

6.11   GRILLED ASPARAGUS

Ready in about: 20 minutes - Servings: 4 - Difficulty: easy

Ingredients:

- 1 lb. of fresh asparagus spears, trimmed.
- Salt and pepper according to taste.
- 1 tbsp. of olive oil.

Instructions:

1. Preheat the grill to high.

2. Apply a thin layer of olive oil to the asparagus spears. To taste, season with pepper and salt.

3. Grill for 2 to 3 minutes over a high flame or until optimal tenderness is reached.

6.12   WARM GRILLED PEACH AND KALE SALAD

Ready in about: 8 hours and 30 minutes - Servings: 4 - Difficulty: hard

Ingredients:

For dressing:

- ¼ cup of apple cider vinegar.
- 2 tbsp. of vegetable oil.
- ½ tsp. of freshly grated ginger.
- 1 medium red bell pepper, chopped.
- ¼ cup of chopped yellow onion.
- 2 tbsp. of honey.
- ½ tsp. of garlic paste.

For salad:

- 2 peaches, each cut into 8 wedges.
- ⅓ cup goat cheese.
- 1 tbsp. of vegetable oil.
- ½ lb. of kale leaves, veins removed.
- Salt and pepper according to taste.

Instructions

1. In a container with a lid, mix the red bell pepper, onion, vinegar, oil, ginger, honey, and garlic paste. Cover the pan, mix it up, then chill the dressing for 8 hours overnight.

2. Preheat an outdoor grill to medium-high heat and spray the grate gently with oil.

3. Put peaches and kale on a grill that has been preheated. Toss kale pretty much continuously for 5 minutes or until softened and finely charred around the ends. Cook peaches for about 3 minutes per side, before grill marks emerge.

4. Toss the cooked kale with the dressing in a serving dish. Cooked peaches and goat cheese are served on top. Sprinkle pepper and salt as per taste. Heat the dish before serving.

6.13 GRILLED FAVA BEANS WITH MINT, LEMON ZEST, AND SUMAC

Ready in about: 25 minutes - Servings: 4 - Difficulty: easy

Ingredients:

- Olive oil to coat.
- A pinch salt.
- 20 to 30 fresh Fava beans (in the pod).

For dressing:

- 1 finely minced garlic clove.
- Zest from one medium lemon.
- 1 tsp. of sumac.
- 3 tbsp. of olive oil.
- 1 tbsp. of finely chopped shallot.
- ½ tsp. of salt.

For garnish:

- ¼ cup of Italian parsley.
- A squeeze of lemon (optional)
- ¼ cup of chopped fresh mint.
- ½ tsp. of Aleppo chili or regular chili flakes (optional).

Instructions:

1. Preheat the grill to medium-high temperature.

2. Toss the fava beans in a small amount of olive oil, barely enough to cover them, then season generously with salt.

3. Cover grill and cook each side before deep grill marks appear (about 4 to 5 minutes per side). Allow sure the inner bean is tender with a tester.

4. Spread out on a platter and drizzle with dressing. New mint and parsley, as well as Aleppo chili flakes, are sprinkled on top. Add salt as per taste.

5. Offer a squeeze of lemon if you like them to have a stronger lemon taste.

   Eat with your fingers, grinding out the beans with your jaws, much like edamame.

6.14 GRILLED ROMAINE SALAD WITH CORN, FAVA BEANS, AND AVOCADO

Ready in about: 35 minutes - Servings: 4 - Difficulty: easy

Ingredients:

- Olive oil for brushing.
- ½ lb. of fresh fava beans in pods.
- 1 pint of cherry or grape tomatoes halved.
- 2 romaine hearts, cut in half lengthwise.
- 1 ear corn, shucked.
- 1 lemon halved.
- Fresh herbs (Italian parsley or dill)
- 1 avocado, diced.

For yogurt dill dressing:

- 1 tbsp. of olive oil.
- 1 finely minced clove of garlic.
- ½ cup of plain yogurt.
- ¼ tsp. of salt and pepper, more to taste.
- 1 tbsp. of lemon juice.
- 2 tbsp. of chopped dill.

For lemon dressing:

- 1 tbsp. of sherry vinegar.
- 1 tsp. of agave or honey.
- ½ tsp. of salt.
- 4 tbsp. of olive oil.
- 1 tbsp. of lemon juice.
- 1 fat garlic clove, minced.
- 1 tsp. of sumac (optional).

Instructions:

1. Preheat the grill to medium-high heat.

2. Set aside the dressing components after whisking them together.

3. Season romaine with salt and olive oil, then grill each side quickly (leave the lid open) before nice grill marks emerge. Place these on a platter, a big cutting board, or a baking sheet.

4. Over medium fire, grill the lemon (cut side down), fava beans, and corn on the cob. Shuck and split the fava beans among the romaine wedges once they are soft around 10 minutes. Remove the corn kernels and separate them. Combine the halved cherry tomatoes and sliced avocado in a mixing dish.

5. Squeeze the grilled lemon halves over the salad and drizzle a little dressing on top. Fresh herbs are to be strewn on top before serving.

BURGERS
RECIPES

CHAPTER 7 - BURGERS RECIPES

7.1 BEEF TARTARE BURGER

Ready in about: 30 minutes - Servings: 4 - Difficulty: easy

Ingredients:

- 1 peeled shallot.
- 1 tbsp. of capers.
- ½ cup of chopped fresh parsley.
- 2 tsp. of Worcestershire sauce.
- 1 ½ lb. of chuck or fatty sirloin.
- 1 medium peeled clove of garlic.

- 2 anchovy fillets.
- ½ tsp. of Tabasco sauce.
- Salt and pepper according to taste.
- Lemon slices for garnish (optional).
- Chopped cooked egg, capers, whole anchovies, sweet white onion, fresh parsley

Instructions:

1. The grill rack should be about 4 inches from the flame, and the flame should be medium to high. In a food processor, pulse the beef, garlic, shallot, anchovies, and capers, if using, until roughly ground—not much finer than sliced.

2. Combine it with Worcestershire sauce, parsley, and in a mixing bowl, and Tabasco sauce season with pepper and salt. Gently combine, then taste it and change seasonings as required. Shape the beef into 4 or more burgers, using as little pressure as possible to prevent compressing it.

3. Grill for 3 minutes per side and another minute per side for each level of doneness after that.

4. If needed, top with chopped capers, egg, anchovies, parsley, onion, and lemon.

7.2   THE PERFECT BASIC BURGER

Ready in about: 35 minutes - Servings: 4 - Difficulty: easy

Ingredients:

- ½ tsp. of salt.

- 1 egg.

- ½ tsp. of ground black pepper.

- ½ cup of fine dry bread crumbs.

- 1 lb. of ground beef.

Instructions

1. Preheat the outdoor grill to high heat and spray the grate gently with oil.

2. Whisk together the egg, pepper, and salt in a medium mixing bowl. Combine the ground beef with the bread crumbs in a mixing bowl. Mix with your hands or a fork until everything is well mixed. Make 4 patties, each around 3/4-inch wide.

3. Place the patties on the grill that has been preheated. Cook for 6 to 8 minutes per side or until ideal doneness is reached.

7.3   CURRY-SPICED LAMB BURGERS

Ready in about: 20 minutes - Servings: 4 - Difficulty: easy

Ingredients:

- 1 medium (or half large) onion, chopped.

- 1 tsp. of ground coriander.

- ½ tsp. of turmeric.

- Diced mango, red onion, green and red bell pepper, and scallion.

- Lettuce and shredded carrot for garnish (optional).

- 1 ½ lb. of boneless lamb shoulder, cut into chunks.

- 1 fresh chili, seeded and minced.

- 1 tsp. of ground cumin.

- Salt and black pepper according to taste.

Instructions:

1. The heat is supposed to be set to medium-high, and the rack should be about 4-inches away from the flames. Place the onion and lamb in a food processor and process until coarsely ground. Add the chili, coriander, turmeric, and cumin to a bowl and season with pepper and salt. Mix when well, with as minimal handling of the meat as possible. Season with pepper and salt as per the taste. Shape the meat into 4 burgers, using as little pressure to prevent compressing it.

2. Grill for 3 minutes per side or more, until the level of doneness of your preference.

3. If needed, garnish with red and green peppers, diced mango, scallion, and red onion, as well as lettuce and shredded carrot.

7.4   GRILLED CHILI BURGER

Ready in about: 40 minutes. - Servings: 8 - Difficulty: moderate

Ingredients:

- Salt and freshly ground pepper according to taste.
- 1 tsp. of chili powder, or more to taste.
- 4 tsp. of butter, at room temperature.

- 2 lb. of twice-ground round steak.
- 1 finely minced clove of garlic.
- ¼ cup of bread crumbs.

Instructions:

1. Build a charcoal fire. The fire is ready when the coals are hot, and white ash has formed.

2. Combine the meat and the remaining materials in a mixing bowl. Make 8 patties out of the mixture.

3. Grill on both sides when finished to your liking. Serve with relishes on hamburger buns.

7.5 JAPANESE BURGERS WITH WASABI KETCHUP

Ready in about: 30 minutes. - Servings: 4 - Difficulty: easy

Ingredients:

For the wasabi ketchup:

- 2 tbsp. of soy sauce.
- ½ cup of ketchup.

- 1 tbsp. of wasabi paste.

For the burgers:

- ¼ cup of whole milk.
- ½ lb. of ground pork.
- 1 ½ tsp. of soy sauce.
- ¼ tsp. of pepper.
- 4 brioche buns for serving.

- ½ cup panko or other dry bread crumbs.
- ½ lb. of ground sirloin.
- ¼ cup of finely chopped white onion.
- ½ tsp. of salt.
- Sesame oil for coating hands.

Instructions:

1. Whisk together ketchup, wasabi paste, and soy sauce to make the wasabi ketchup.

2. To render the burgers, preheat the grill to medium-high heat. Combine panko and milk in a big mixing bowl and set aside for 2 to 3 minutes.

3. Combine the sirloin, onion, pork, soy sauce, pepper, and salt in a large mixing cup. Knead the meat until it is moist and sticks together, then break it into 4 portions.

4. Apply a light coating of sesame oil to your palms. Roll each piece of meat into a ball with your fingertips, and pat the ball flat with your hands to create a half-inch-thick patty. To prevent the patty from puffing up when grilling, make a small indentation in the middle with the side of your palm.

5. Grill burgers for 10 minutes, turning twice until browned and cooked through with no pink in the center. Allow for a 2-minute rest period. Serve on buns with wasabi ketchup on the side.

7.6   PORTOBELLO MUSHROOM BURGER

Ready in about: 20 minutes - Servings: 4 - Difficulty: easy

Ingredients:

- Extra-virgin olive oil for drizzling.
- 4 large portobello mushrooms.
- Balsamic vinegar, for drizzling.
- Sea salt and freshly ground black pepper.
- Tamari, for drizzling.

For serving:

- Lettuce.
- Sliced red onion.
- 4 hamburger buns, warmed or toasted.
- Sliced tomato.
- Pickles.
- Pesto, Guacamole, or Chipotle Sauce, optional.
- Ketchup, mayo, mustard.

Instructions:

1. Remove the stems from the mushrooms and wipe the caps clean with a wet cloth or paper towel. Drizzle olive oil, tamari, balsamic vinegar, salt, and pepper over the mushrooms on a rimmed plate. Use your hands to coat all sides of the mushrooms.

2. Over medium fire, preheat a grill or grill plate. Place the mushrooms on the grill pan, gill side up. Cook for 5 to 7 minutes on either side or until the mushrooms are soft.

3. Place the mushrooms on the buns and finish with your preferred toppings.

7.7   JUICY HAMBURGERS

Ready in about: 35 minutes - Servings: 8 - Difficulty: easy

Ingredients:

- 1 beaten egg.

- 1 cup of dry bread crumbs.

- 2 tbsp. of Worcestershire sauce.

- 3 tbsp. of evaporated milk.

- 2 lb. of ground beef.

- 2 cloves of garlic, minced.

- 1/8 tsp. of cayenne pepper.

Instructions:

1. Preheat the grill to high.

2. Mix the egg, bread crumbs, ground beef, evaporated milk, cayenne pepper, Worcestershire sauce, and garlic together in a big mixing bowl with your fingertips. Make 8 hamburger patties out of the mixture.

3. Brush oil on the grill grate gently. Grill the burger patties for about 5 minutes a side or until well baked.

7.8   SALMON BURGERS

Ready in about: 20 minutes - Servings: 4 - Difficulty: easy

Ingredients:

- 2 tsp. of Dijon mustard.

- ½ cup of coarse bread crumb.

- Salt and freshly ground black pepper as per your taste.

- Tabasco sauce.

- 1 ½ lb. of skinless, boneless salmon.

- 2 shallots, cut into chunks.

- 1 tbsp. of capers, drained.

- Lemon wedges.

Instructions:

1. Cut the salmon into big pieces and place around ¼ of it, along with the mustard, in a food processor. Turn the machine on and let it operate until the mixture becomes pasty, stopping to scrub down the sides if possible.

2. Add the shallots and remaining salmon to the puree. Make sure to slice and mix well.

3. No piece should be greater than a quarter-inches in diameter, and the mixture should not be too fine.

4. Scrape the mixture into a dish and whisk in the capers, bread crumbs, and a pinch of pepper and salt by the side. Get 4 burgers out of the mixture.

5. Grill over medium-high heat for around 4 minutes, or until the first side has firmed up; switch and grill for another minute or 2. Make a quick cut and look inside and see if it's finished. Take caution not to overcook the food. Serve with lemon wedges and Tabasco or your favorite dressing on a bed of vegetables, on buns, or on their own.

7.9   TURKEY AND VEGETABLE BURGERS

Ready in about: 1 hour and 30 minutes - Servings: 6 - Difficulty: moderate

Ingredients:

- 1 ½ cup of finely diced onion.

- Salt according to taste.

- 2/3 cup finely grated carrot (1 large carrot).

- 1 tbsp. of prepared barbecue sauce.

- 1 tbsp. of extra virgin olive oil.

- ½ cup of finely diced red bell pepper.

- 1 large clove of garlic, minced.

- 1 ¼ lb. lean ground turkey breast.

- 1 tbsp. of ketchup.

- Whole-grain hamburger buns.

- Freshly ground pepper according to taste.

Instructions:

1. In a medium skillet, melt the olive oil over medium heat and add the onion. Cook, occasionally stirring, for 3 minutes or until it starts to soften, then season with red pepper and a sufficient pinch of salt. Cook, often stirring, for around 5 minutes, or until vegetables are soft. Cook for another minute or 2, constantly stirring, until the carrots have softened somewhat and the mixture is fragrant. Remove the pan from the heat.

2. Mash the ground turkey with a fork in a wide mixing dish. If required, season with ¼ tsp. of kosher salt and season with barbecue sauce, ketchup, and pepper to taste. Combine the sautéed vegetables and stir well. Make 6 patties, each about 3/4 inches thick. If necessary, chill for 1 hour to make dealing easier.

3. Preheat the grill to medium-high heat. Patties should be baked for 4 minutes on either side. Serve with your favorite condiments on whole-grain buns.

7.10 DOUBLE RL RANCH BURGER

Ready in about: 1 hour and 30 minutes - Servings: 8 - Difficulty: moderate

Ingredients:

For Ralph's special sauce:

- ⅓ cup of ketchup.
- 1 tbsp. of cornichons, finely chopped.
- 1 tsp. of Worcestershire sauce.
- ½ tsp. of onion powder.
- Kosher salt and black pepper.

- Half cup of mayonnaise.
- 2 tbsp. of sweet relish.
- 1 tbsp. of finely chopped red onion.
- ½ tsp. of garlic powder.
- ¼ tsp. of hot sauce.

For burgers:

- Kosher salt.
- 8 sesame of buns, toasted.
- Green leaf lettuce, sliced red onion, sliced tomato, and sliced pickles (for serving).

- 3 lb. of ground beef chuck.
- 8 oz. of clothbound cheddar, thinly sliced.
- 16 slices of bacon, cooked.

Instructions:

For Ralph's special sauce:

1. In a shallow mixing bowl, combine the ketchup, mayonnaise, relish, cornichons, garlic powder, Worcestershire sauce, onion powder, onion, and hot sauce; season with pepper and salt.

2. Sauce may be made up to 2 days ahead of time. Cover and put aside to relax.

For burgers:

1. Preheat the grill to medium-high. Cut the beef into 8 halves.

2. Work with one part at a time and carefully mould it into a circular patty, taking caution not to over-pack the meat. Lightly push down on the patty to flatten it, then use your thumb to create a tiny indentation in the middle.

3. Season all sides of the patties generously with salt and then grill for 5 minutes. Toss in the cheese and serve. Cover grill and cook for another 5 minutes or until the cheese is melted and patties are cooked. Allow 5 minutes to rest on a platter.

4. Now assemble your burger and enjoy!

7.11   HOMEMADE BLACK BEAN VEGGIE BURGERS

Ready in about: 35 minutes - Servings: 4 - Difficulty: easy

Ingredients:

- Half green bell pepper.

- 3 cloves of garlic, peeled.

- 1 tbsp. of chili powder.

- 1 (16 oz) can of black beans, drained and rinsed.

- Half onion, cut into wedges.

- 1 egg.

- 1 tbsp. of cumin.

- Half cup of bread crumbs.

- 1 tsp. of hot sauce or Thai chili sauce.

Instructions:

1. Preheat an outdoor grill to full heat and gently oil a sheet of aluminum foil.

2. Mash black beans with a fork in a medium bowl until thick and pasty.

3. Finely cut the onion, bell pepper, and garlic in a food processor. And add it to the mashed beans.

4. Combine the egg, cumin, chili powder, and chili sauce in a small bowl.

5. In a mixing bowl, beat the eggs and add them to the mashed beans. Bread crumbs can be used before the paste is moist and sticks together. Create 4 patties out of the mixture.

6. Place patties on foil and grill for 8 minutes on either side.

7.12 GOURMET GRILLING BURGERS

Ready in about: 40 minutes - Servings: 8 - Difficulty: easy

Ingredients:

- ½ lb. of bulk Italian sausage.
- 2 Anaheim chili peppers, chopped.
- ¾ lb. of Muenster cheese, shredded.
- 1 tbsp. of Worcestershire sauce.
- Salt and pepper according to taste.

- 2 lb. of lean ground beef.
- Half large red onion, chopped.
- 3 cloves of garlic, minced.
- 1 egg.
- 1 tsp. of chili powder.

Instructions:

1. Preheat an outdoor grill to medium-high heat and spray the grate gently with oil.

2. In a mixing dish, add the sausage, ground beef, onion, chili pepper, Worcestershire sauce, garlic, Muenster cheese, egg, and chili powder. Season with pepper and salt to taste, then combine once more. Make 8 patties out of the beef mixture.

3. On a preheated grill, cook for around 7 minutes per side until the burgers are no longer pink in the middle. The temperature should read 160° F on an instant-read thermometer inserted into the middle (70° C).

7.13 THAI TURKEY BURGERS WITH ASIAN SLAW

Ready in about: 45 minutes - Servings: 3 to 4 - Difficulty: moderate

Ingredients:

For turkey burger:

- 3 tbsp. of diced shallot or red onion.
- 2 finely minced garlic cloves or 1 tsp. of granulated garlic.
- 2 tbsp. of chopped red basil or Thai basil, mint or cilantro.
- 1 chopped scallion.
- 1 tbsp. of fish sauce or sub soy sauce.

- ¼ tsp. of white pepper.
- 1 lb. ground turkey.
- 1 ½ tsp. of fresh grated or chopped ginger.
- 1 tbsp. of finely chopped lemongrass.
- 1 tsp. of lime zest.
- 1 jalapeño, seeded, finely chopped.

- 1 tsp. of sugar.

For crunchy Asian slaw:

- 1 cup of purple cabbage, shredded.

- 2 tbsp. of rice wine vinegar or lime juice.

- 1 cup of grated carrots.

- 1 thinly sliced scallion.

- 1 tbsp. of olive oil.

- ¼ tsp. of pepper and salt each.

- 1 tsp. of sugar.

For spicy aioli:

- 2 tbsp. of chili garlic sauce or sriracha.

- ¼ cup of mayo or tartar sauce.

- Optional Additions—Cucumber Ribbons, Toasted Buns, pickled red onions (yum), spicy greens like avocado, watercress, or sprouts, Pickled radishes.

Instructions:

1. Preheat the grill to medium-high temperature.

2. In a medium mixing bowl, combine all the ingredients of the burger and blend well with your fingertips. Shape 3 1-inch-thick burgers with wet palms. Put in the fridge on a tray.

3. In a medium mixing bowl, combine the slaw ingredients.

4. In a small bowl, combine the ingredients for the spicy aioli.

5. Grill patties for 4 to 5 minutes on either side on a well-oiled preheated grill until golden.

6. The buns may be toasted or fried.

7. On the bottom bun, spread aioli, then top with the patty, slaw, cucumber ribbons (optional), more aioli, and the top bun.

7.14 HEALTHY BURGER BOWLS

Ready in about: 30 minutes - Servings: 2 - Difficulty: easy

Ingredients:

For burger patties:

- Lamb, chicken, beef, veggie, turkey, or vegan.

For grill veggies:

- 1 onion, bell pepper, zucchini, tomato, eggplant, or asparagus.

For salad:

- 2 large handfuls of fresh greens—spinach, arugula, mesclun, baby kale, or any other salad greens.

For fresh veggies:

- Grated carrot, cucumber, grated beet, radish, tomatoes, shredded cabbage, sprouts, avocado, or any other veggie of your choice.

For optional additions:

- Nuts, seeds, fermented things like kimchi or sauerkraut, pickled shallots or onions.

For dressing:

- Caesar, green goddess, balsamic, gorganzola, tahini, or simply olive oil and lemon.

Instructions:

1. Preheat the grill to medium-high temperature.

2. Prepare the burgers as well as the vegetables.

3. Grill burgers and any other grill-able vegetables, then lower the heat after they've been labelled.

4. Assemble bowls with veggies, greens, grilled veggies, and burgers, then drizzle with dressing and any optional toppings.

5. Enjoy your burger in a bowl.

CHAPTER 08

POULTRY RECIPES

CHAPTER 8 - POULTRY RECIPES

8.1   CHICKEN BREASTS MARINATED IN BASIL OIL WITH TOMATO AND RED ONION SALAD

Ready in about: 40 minutes (Basil oil excluded) - Servings: 4 - Difficulty: easy

Ingredients:

For basil oil:

- 2 cups plus 7 tbsp. of extra virgin olive oil.

- 2 bunches of fresh basil stems on.

For chicken:

- 4 tsp. of basil oil.

- 1 thinly sliced red onion.

- 12 fresh basil leaves, cut across into thin strips.

- 4 boneless, skinless chicken breast halves.

- 2 large, thinly sliced tomatoes.

- Salt and freshly ground pepper to taste.

Instructions:

For basil oil:

1. A big pot of water should be brought to a boil. 30 seconds after adding the basil, blanch it for 30 seconds. Drain and scrub until cool under cold running water. Drain and thoroughly rinse basil. Add 5 tbsp. of olive oil to a food processor and process until it's smooth. Scrape the mixture into a clean glass container and add 2 cups of olive oil. Shake well before storing for 1 to 2 days in a cool and dry place.

2. Using a fine-mesh sieve, strain the oil. To dampen a coffee filter, pour the remaining 2 tsp. of olive oil into it. Place the filter inside the clean glass jar's bottom. Cover the filter with basil oil and let it drip into a container. Continue pouring and letting the oil trickle into the filter until all of it has soaked through. It should be kept in the refrigerator.

For chicken:

1. 1 tsp. basil oil, apply it with a brush to chicken breasts. Allow for half an hour of resting time. Prepare a grill by preheating it. Grill for around 4 to 5 minutes every side on the grill before the chicken is cooked through. Chicken should be sliced and brushed with 1 tsp. of oil.

2. In the middle of all the 4 bowls, place half of the onions and tomatoes. Then pour ¼ tsp. of basil oil over each one and season with pepper and salt. Layers can be repeated. Chicken slices can be fanned out throughout the salad. Sprinkle basil strips on top of the chicken and salad.

8.2 GRILLED BACON-WRAPPED CHICKEN TENDERS

Ready in about: 40 minutes - Servings: 4 - Difficulty: easy

Ingredients:

- 1 tbsp. of BBQ rub.
- 8 chicken tenders.
- 8 slices center cut bacon.
- 1 tsp. of water.
- 2 tbsp. of honey.

Instructions:

1. Preheat the grill to medium heat and spray the grate gently with oil.

2. Rub BBQ rub on chicken. Wrap 2 bacon strips around each tender, tucking the ends in to protect.

3. In a tiny bowl, mix water and honey. Then set aside.

4. Reduce the heat to medium-low temperature and put the chicken tenders on the grill. Close the lid and then grill for around 15 minutes, flipping every 3 minutes until the bacon changes its color to brown and the chicken reaches an inside temperature of 165° F. Increase the heat for the last 2 minutes of cooking for crispier bacon.

5. Place the tenders on a low heat setting and brush with the honey mixture. Serve directly on a tray.

8.3 GRILLED CHICKEN WITH MEDITERRANEAN FLAVORS

Ready in about: 45 minutes - Servings: 4 - Difficulty: moderate

Ingredients:

- 1 tsp. of thyme leaves.
- ½ tsp. of chopped lavender leaves.
- Extra virgin olive oil as needed.
- 8 bay leaves.
- Salt and freshly ground black pepper.

- 1 tsp. of chopped rosemary leaves.
- ¼ cup of roughly chopped parsley.
- 8 chicken drumsticks or thighs.
- 2 lemons, cut into quarters.

Instructions:

1. Light a wood fire or charcoal, or switch on the gas grill. The fire should only be reasonably high, and the rack should be 4 to 6 inches away from the heat source.

2. Integrate pepper, salt, rosemary, thyme, parsley, and lavender in a shallow cup. To create a paste, apply sufficiently olive oil to make a paste. Loosen the skin of the chicken and slip a bay leaf between the skin and the meat, then stuff a part of the herb mixture between the skin and the meat. Return the skin to the meat and season with pepper and salt.

3. Place the chicken skin side up on the grill's coolest section. Turn the chicken over after the fat has melted a little. Shift the chicken to the hottest section of the grill after around 20 minutes, brush with olive oil, and grill until the meat is cooked and the skin is well browned.

4. Serve with lemon wedges on the side.

8.4 GRILLED CHICKEN WITH CHIPOTLE SAUCE

Ready in about: 45 minutes. - Servings: 4 - Difficulty: moderate

Ingredients:

- 1 medium-sized chopped white onion.

- 2 cups of cored and chopped tomatoes.

- 8 chicken thighs, whole legs, or drumsticks.

- 2 tbsp. of lard or neutral oil, like canola or corn.

- 2 dried chipotle chilies, as per your taste.

- Salt and pepper as per taste.

- 2 cloves of garlic halved.

- Lime wedges.

- Freshly chopped cilantro leaves.

Instructions:

1. Preheat a gas grill or start a charcoal or wood fire; the fire should be relatively high, with part of the grill cooler than the rest and the rack 4 to 6 inches from the heat source.

2. In a medium saucepan or skillet, melt the lard or oil over medium flame. When the pan is heated, add the onion and cook, stirring regularly, until it starts to brown, around 5 to 10 minutes. Stir in the tomatoes, chilies, and half a cup of water. Shift the heat such that the mixture simmers slowly and gradually. Cook for 15 minutes, stirring regularly until the chilies are soft and the tomatoes have broken up. If required, season with pepper and salt. When the chipotle sauce is ready, let it cool for a few minutes before cutting the stems and pureeing the mixture in a blender.

3. Meanwhile, rub the chicken with the cut side of garlic cloves, drizzle with oil, and season with pepper and salt to taste.

4. Place the chicken skin side up on the grill's coolest section. Turn the chicken over after the fat has made a little. Shift the chicken to the hottest section of the grill after around 20 minutes. Brush all sides of the chicken with chipotle sauce when it's almost cooked, then simmer for another minute or 2. Serve with cilantro and lime wedges on the side.

8.5 GAYLORD'S TANDOORI CHICKEN

Ready in about: 45 minutes - Servings: 4 to 8 - Difficulty: moderate

Ingredients:

- 2 cups of plain yogurt.

- ½ tsp. of freshly ground black pepper.

- ¼ tsp. of ground cloves.

- 1 tsp. of grated fresh ginger or a ½ tsp. of dried ginger.

- 1/8 to ¼ tsp. of cayenne pepper.

- ½ tsp. of ground cardamom.

- 1 whole chicken (3-4 lb.)

- ½ tsp. of ground cumin.

- ¼ tsp. of freshly grated nutmeg.

- ½ tsp. of ground coriander.

- 1 clove garlic, minced.

- Salt as per taste.

- ½ cup of chopped white onion.

- ½ tsp. of loosely packed saffron threads, or ¼ tsp. of powdered saffron.

- 2 tbsp. of milk.

Instructions:

1. Every chicken's tiny wingtips should be cut off and discarded. Take the skin off the chicken with your fingertips and discard it.

2. Create short gashes through the grain on both sides of chicken breast and legs with a small knife.

3. Take yogurt, black pepper, cumin, nutmeg, coriander, cloves, ginger, cayenne pepper, garlic, cardamom, salt to taste, onion and mix in a food processor. Get a fine liquid out of it.

4. Apply the mixture to the chicken. Switch the chicken over and cover both edges. Refrigerate for at least 24 hours after covering.

5. 1 hour before serving, remove the chicken from the yogurt mixture.

6. Preheat the oven to 500° F. A barbecue grill should be preheated.

7. In a tiny saucepan, heat the milk and add the saffron. Take the pan off the heat and set it aside for 10 minutes.

8. Using a spoon, uniformly distribute the saffron mixture over the chicken.

9. Heavy-duty foil can be used to line a baking dish. Place the chicken with breast facing up.

10. Bake for 20 minutes in the oven.

11. Chicken can be cut into serving sections. Place them on the grill and cook them for a few minutes on both sides.

8.6   GRILLED TABASCO CHICKEN

Ready in about: 40 minutes - Servings: 6 - Difficulty: moderate

Ingredients:

- 1 tbsp. of soy sauce.
- 6 chicken legs.
- 1 tbsp. of ketchup.

- 1 tbsp. of Tabasco sauce.
- 1 tbsp. of cider vinegar.

Instructions:

1. Trim the tips of the drumsticks and cut halfway into the joint, linking each leg's thigh and drumstick.

2. In a tray, mix ketchup, soy sauce, vinegar, Tabasco, and roll chicken legs in the marinade.

3. Cook for about 10 minutes, skin side down, on the rack of a hot grill about 10 inches from the blaze. Cook for around 10 minutes on the other side after flipping the wings. Cook them for another 10 minutes with the skin side down.

4. Remove the legs from the heat and put them aside to rest for 5 minutes before eating.

8.7   JALAPEÑO STUFFED GAME HENS

Ready in about: 45 minutes Servings: 4 - Difficulty: moderate

Ingredients:

- Salt and freshly ground pepper to taste.
- 6 slices of bacon.

- 2 Cornish game hens.
- 4 jalapeños, halved and seeded.

Instructions:

1. Heat a grill until it is really hot.

2. Season the hens with pepper and salt before serving. Place 4 jalapeño halves in each hen's cavity. Wrap 3 slices of bacon over each hen's breast, securing the bacon with toothpicks submerged in water.

3. Place the hens on the grill and cook for around 10 minutes, or until well browned on all sides.

4. Cover grill and cook for around 40 minutes, rotating once, until hens are cooked through.

5. Remove toothpicks, cut hens lengthwise in half, divide across 4 dishes, and serve right away.

8.8   POULET GRILLE AU GINGEMBRE (GRILLED CHICKEN WITH GINGER)

Ready in about: 35 minutes (marination time excluded) - Servings: 2 - Difficulty: moderate

Ingredients:

- 1 tbsp. of finely chopped ginger.
- ¼ cup of fresh lemon juice.
- 1 bay leaf, broken into small pieces.
- 1 chicken.
- 1 tsp. of minced garlic.
- 2 tbsp. of olive oil.
- ½ tsp. of dried thyme.
- Melted butter.
- Salt and freshly ground pepper to taste.

Instructions:

1. Place the chicken in a bowl.

2. In a shallow mixing bowl, combine the garlic, thyme, lemon, ginger, bay, oil, and pepper and salt as per taste.

3. Pour the marinade over the chicken and refrigerate for around 3 to 4 hours.

4. Preheat the grill to medium-high temperature.

5. Place the chicken on the grill with the skin side down. Cook until the skin is well browned, then flip. Continue to cook, turning the chicken every 20 to 25 minutes or until finished. Serve with a scoop of melted butter on top.

8.9   STICKY BARBECUE CHICKEN

Ready in about: 35 minutes (marination time excluded) - Servings: 8 to 10 - Difficulty: moderate

Ingredients:

For barbecue seasoning:

- 2 tbsp. of light brown sugar.
- ¼ cup of smoked paprika.
- 2 tsp. of chili powder.
- 1 ½ tsp. of cayenne pepper.
- 2 tsp. of garlic powder.

For chicken:

- Zest and juice of 2 lemons.
- 5 tbsp. of barbecue seasoning, divided.
- 1 small onion, finely chopped.
- 2 tbsp. of light brown sugar.
- 2 tbsp. of apple cider vinegar.
- 1 tbsp. of Dijon mustard.
- 1 tbsp. of Worcestershire sauce.
- 12 skin-on, bone-in chicken thighs.
- 4 tsp. of Diamond Crystal or 2 ½ tsp. of Morton kosher salt.
- 1 tbsp. of vegetable oil.
- 3 finely chopped garlic cloves.
- ¾ cup of ketchup.
- 2 tbsp. of non-sulfured blackstrap molasses.
- 1 tbsp. of Louisiana hot sauce.

Instructions:

For barbecue seasoning:

1. In a shallow mixing bowl, add paprika, brown sugar, chili powder, garlic powder, and cayenne. It will make approximately half a cup.

2. Seasoning may be prepared up to a month ahead of time. Store in an airtight container at room temperature.

For chicken:

1. In a broad mixing bowl, toss the chicken with the lemon juice and zest to cover. Season with salt and 4 tbsp. seasoning, tossing to cover uniformly. Allow at least 2 hours and up to 12 hours for chilling.

2. In a medium saucepan, heat 1 tbsp. of oil over medium-high heat. Cook, stirring regularly, until garlic and onion are soft, around 3 minutes. Cook, stirring continuously, for 2 minutes, or until brown sugar makes a shade deeper. Add the remaining 1 tsp. of seasoning and cook, constantly stirring, for 30 seconds, or until fragrant. Cook, stirring continuously until the ketchup has marginally darkened in color, around 2 minutes. In a large mixing bowl, combine the vinegar, molasses, mustard, chili sauce, and Worcestershire sauce. Bring to a boil over high heat, constantly stirring for 2 minutes. Allow 5 minutes for cooling. Purée in a blender until almost smooth. Set aside the sauce.

3. Prepare a grill for medium-high indirect heat. Grates can be lightly oiled. 5 minutes over direct heat, rotating every minute before the chicken is browned on all sides.

4. Move chicken to indirect fire, cover, and barbecue, rotating every 5 minutes or so before the thermometer inserted into the thickest section of the thighs reports 145° F for about 20 minutes. Uncover grill and cook for another 10 to 15 minutes, basting with reserved sauce and rotating periodically, before thermometer reads 165° F.

8.10 GRILLED BUTTERFLIED CHICKEN WITH LEMONGRASS SAUCE

Ready in about: 1 hour (marination time excluded) - Servings: 4 - Difficulty: hard

Ingredients:

For sauce:

- 3 finely chopped lemongrass stalks.

- 2 finely chopped garlic cloves.

- 6 thinly sliced scallions.

- 1 2-inch piece of finely chopped ginger.

- ½ cup of vegetable oil.

- Kosher salt.

- ½ tsp. of Aji-No-Moto umami seasoning.

For chicken:

- 1 tbsp. of cumin seeds.

- 2 tsp. of coriander seeds.

- ⅓ to 4 lbs. of a whole chicken, backbone removed.

- 3 tbsp. of vegetable oil.

- Kosher salt.

Instructions:

For the sauce:

1. In a medium mixing dish, combine scallions, ginger, lemongrass, and garlic. In a small saucepan, heat the oil over high heat until it is hot but not burning, around 2 minutes. Pour the scallion mixture on top. Allow 5 minutes to rest, often stirring to avoid burning the aromatics. Season with salt and Aji-No-Moto seasoning.

2. Sauce may be made up to 2 days ahead of time. Cover and put aside to relax.

For chicken:

1. In a small dry skillet over medium heat, toast coriander and cumin seeds, shaking periodically, until fragrant and slightly darkened in color, around 3 minutes. Allow cooling before transferring to a mortar and pestle or spice mill. Move spice mixture to a small bowl after finely grinding.

2. Place the chicken on a cutting board, skin side up. Push forcefully on the breastbone with your hands to flatten the breast; you can hear a snap. Place the chicken on a wide-rimmed baking dish, skin side up.

3. Season all sides generously with salt, then scatter spice mix all around, making sure to get into any nook and cranny. Underneath the breast, tuck the wings. Chill for at least 4 hours or up to 48 hours.

4. Allow 1 hour for the chicken to come to room temperature before grilling. Drizzle some oil on everything and wipe it down.

5. Prepare a barbecue for indirect medium-high temperature. Place the chicken on the grate, skin side down, over the indirect fire. Place a vent over the chicken to pull heat up and over it. Cook for around 20 minutes on the grill before the skin is finely browned.

6. Cook, wrapped, for another 20 to 25 minutes, or until the skin is deep golden brown and crisp and the thermometer inserted into the thickest portion of the breast registers 160° F. Until slicing, move the chicken to a chopping board and let it rest for at least 15 minutes. Serve with rice and lemongrass sauce.

8.11 ROTISSERIE CHICKEN

Ready in about: 1 hour and 30 minutes - Servings: 4 - Difficulty: hard

Ingredients:

- 1 tbsp. of salt.

- ¼ tbsp. of ground black pepper.

- 1 (3 lb.) whole chicken.

- ¼ cup of melted butter.

- 1 tbsp. of paprika.

Instructions:

1. Using a pinch of salt, season the interior of the chicken. Set the grill to maximum and put the chicken on a rotisserie. Cook for around 10 to 15 minutes before serving.

2. During this time, easily combine the butter, 1 tbsp. of salt, paprika, and pepper in a small mixing bowl. Reduce to medium-low heat and baste the chicken with the butter mixture. Shut the lid and cook for around 1 to 1 hour and 30 minutes, basting regularly, before the internal temperature of the thigh with a meat thermometer approaches 180° F.

3. Remove the chicken from the rotisserie and set aside for 15 to 20 minutes before slicing and serving.

8.12 BAJA GRILLED CHICKEN TACOS

Ready in about: 1 hour and 10 minutes - Servings: 6 - Difficulty: hard

Ingredients:

- 1 tsp. of dried Mexican oregano.

- 1 tsp. of garlic powder.

- ¼ tsp. of cayenne pepper.

- 1 tsp. of olive oil.

- 1 tsp. of cumin.

- 1 tp. of sazon seasoning.

- 1 tsp. of salt.

- ¼ cup of fresh lime juice.

- 1 lb. of skinless, boneless chicken thighs.

- 1 (10 oz.) package corn tortillas, or as needed.

- Canola oil cooking spray.

Instructions:

1. In a wide mixing bowl, add oregano, cumin, sazon, garlic powder, cinnamon, and cayenne pepper. To produce the marinade, combine the lime juice and olive oil in a mixing bowl. Refrigerate for around 30 minutes to 12 hours after adding the chicken.

2. Preheat an outdoor grill to medium heat and spray the grate gently with oil. Grill marinated chicken for 8 to 10 minutes each side, or until no longer pink at the bone and juices run clear. Move the chicken to a bowl and shred it with forks.

3. Spray the tortillas with canola oil and cook for 45 seconds on each. To stay wet, switch to a plate and cover with a paper towel. And shredded chicken on foot.

8.13 GRILLED CHICKEN SHAWARMA

Ready in about: 30 minutes - Servings: 6 - Difficulty: easy

Ingredients:

- 2 lbs. to 2 ¼ lb. chicken thigh.

Shawarma marinade:

- 2 tbsp. of ground coriander.
- 2 tsp. of kosher salt.
- ¼ tsp. of cayenne pepper.
- 1 tsp. of ground ginger.
- 2 tsp. of allspice.

- 2 tbsp. of ground cumin.
- 8 minced garlic cloves.
- 6 tbsp. of olive oil.
- 2 tsp. of turmeric.
- 1 tsp. of ground black pepper.

Instructions:

1. Combine all marinade ingredients in a bowl and stir to combine, or pulse to produce a paste in a food processor.

2. Marinade the chicken on both sides and set aside for 20 minutes (or up to 1 day or 2 refrigerated).

3. Grill the chicken on a preheated grill over medium-high heat, sealed, for around 8 minutes per side, until both sides have good grill marks. Transfer the chicken to a cooler section of the grill or finish cooking it in a 350° F oven for around 10 minutes or until fully cooked.

4. Chicken shawarma may be eaten with Israeli salad, rice, and onions, or pita bread and tzatziki.

8.14 GRILLED CHICKEN WITH ITALIAN SALSA VERDE

Ready in about: 45 minutes - Servings: 4 - Difficulty: moderate

Ingredients:

- 4 to 6 pieces of chicken, either thighs or breasts.
- Kosher salt and pepper according to taste.

For Italian-style salsa verde:

- 2 garlic cloves.
- 2 tsp. of lemon zest.
- 1 tbsp. of caper juice.
- 1 cup of Italian parsley.
- ⅛ cup lemon juice.
- 2 tbsp. of capers.
- 1 anchovy.
- ¼ tsp. of pepper and salt, or to taste.
- ⅓ cup of olive oil plus more for cooking.

For Tuscan tomato salad:

- 2 tbsp. of olive oil.
- 2 lbs. of heirloom tomatoes.
- 2 tbsp. of balsamic vinegar.
- A handful of herbs.
- Pepper and salt according to taste.

Instructions:

1. Preheat the grill to medium-high temperature and the oven to 350° F.

2. Season the chicken on both sides with pepper and salt.

3. Grill chicken on a well-oiled grill over medium heat until healthy grill marks show on all sides and the grill is fully covered. Place the chicken in a warm oven, uncovered, for 10 to 15 minutes, depending on the cut of chicken. Hold the burgers on the grill in a cooler place until they're fully done.

4. Create the Italian type salsa verde while the chicken is grilling.

5. In a food processor, mix all of the ingredients and process about 12 to 15 cycles, or until sliced and only mixed. Put all in a bowl and set it aside.

6. Cut various ripe tomatoes and arrange them on a platter to create the tomato salad. Drizzle with extra virgin olive oil, balsamic vinegar, and season with pepper and salt. For added flavor, scatter fresh herbs on top.

7. Distribute the chicken and tomato salad among the plates and finish with a drizzle of salsa verde.

CHAPTER 09

MEAT RECIPES

CHAPTER 9 - MEAT RECIPES

9.1   GREMLIN GRILL'S PRIME RIB

Ready in about: 3 hours and 30 minutes, plus overnight refrigeration - Servings: 10 to 14-

Difficulty: hard

Ingredients:

For Greek seasoning blend:

2 tsp. of dried oregano.

1 ½ tsp. of garlic powder.

1 tsp. of freshly ground black pepper.

1 tsp. of dried parsley flakes.

½ tsp. of ground nutmeg.

1 tsp. of salt.

1 ½ tsp. of onion powder.

1 tsp. of cornstarch.

1 tsp. of beef-flavored bouillon granules.

½ tsp. of ground cinnamon.

For rib:

- 1 cup of cherry coke.

- 1 tbsp. of kosher salt.

- Greek seasoning blend.

- 1 tsp. of dried thyme.

- 1 cup of olive oil.

- 2 tbsp. of Worcestershire sauce.

- 1 tbsp. of ground black pepper.

- 1 tbsp. of dried oregano.

- 1 tsp. of onion powder.

- 10 lb. of boneless prime rib.

- 2 tbsp. of minced garlic.

Instructions:

For Greek seasoning blend:

1. In a mixing bowl, combine all ingredients and put them in an airtight jar. Keep in a dry place.

For rib:

1. Mix olive oil, salt, cherry coke, Worcestershire sauce, pepper, and 1 tbsp. of Greek seasoning blend in a mixing bowl.

2. Combine oregano, onion powder, thyme, and garlic in a large mixing bowl. Mix well. In a big roasting pan, place the meat. Add the marinade and rub it into the meat, rotating it to evenly cover it. Seal well the meat and marinade in an extra-large Ziploc plastic bag. Refrigerate for a day.

3. To start, create a charcoal fire. Cover the grill and place the grill rack over the coals.

4. Add the meat to a big disposable aluminum roasting pan with tiny gaps. Place the pan over the grill's center, cover it, and change the airflow, so it's partially accessible. Insert a thermometer through a ventilation hole in the grill cover to verify the temperature, which should be about 225° F. To keep the temperature in check, adjust the ventilation.

5. Cook for 2 hours and 30 minutes to 3 hours, or before an instant-read thermometer placed in the middle reads 130° F. Add coals on either side of the fire every 30 minutes or as needed to keep it burning. To keep the fire burning, add more wet wood chips as needed.

6. Remove the meat from the pan and cover it in foil. Enable for room temperature before refrigerating for at least 2 to 3 hours or overnight.

7. Light a charcoal fire to serve. Scatter the white coal over the rim of the grill. Remove inch-thick steaks from the meat and season to taste with the remaining Greek seasoning blend. Grill until done to your liking. Serve right away.

9.2   BARBECUED STEAK AU POIVRE

Ready in about: 1 hour - Servings: 6 to 10 - Difficulty: moderate

Ingredients:

- 1 tbsp. of coarse salt.

- ¼ cup of finely chopped shallots.

- 3 (1 ½-lb.) boneless shell steaks, trimmed.

- ¼ cup of crushed black peppercorns.

- ½ cup of dry red wine.

- 4 tbsp. (half stick) of non-salted butter.

- ½ cup of beef stock, homemade or canned.

Instructions:

1. Coarsely salt the steaks. Place crushed peppercorns on the surface and coat steaks on all sides with them.

2. Grill the steaks for a total of 20 minutes. Cook for about 4 minutes on one side, then flip and cook the other side for another 4 minutes. Standing steaks on their sides for many minutes can even sear the smooth rim. Continue spinning until the steaks are cooked to your taste.

3. When the steaks are grilling, mix shallot, red wine, and beef stock in a saucepan. Reduce to 1/3 of the initial volume over medium-high temperature. Transfer the cooked steaks to a serving platter that is still soft. Pour the sauce over the steaks after swirling in the fat. In a platter, slice the steaks on the bias, enabling the juices to blend with the sauce.

9.3   GRILLED FLANK STEAK

Ready in about: 15 minutes plus 2 hours refrigeration - Servings: 6 - Difficulty: moderate

Ingredients:

- ½ cup bourbon.

- 1 ½-lb. of flank steak.

- ½ cup soy sauce.

Instructions:

1. To create a marinade, add soy sauce, bourbon, and ½ a cup of water in a small bowl. Fill a gallon-size self-sealing food storage bag halfway with marinade. Place the steak in the bag and spin it many times to cover the whole cut. Marinate for 2 hours in the refrigerator, rotating the steak once after 1 hour. Remove the steak from the marinade and wipe it dry with paper towels.

2. Make a fire in the grill. Grill steak for 4 minutes on one side for rare, 5 minutes for medium-rare until flames have died down and coals are glowing. Turn the steak and cook for another 3 or 4 minutes, or until done to your liking.

3. Transfer the steak to a cutting board, cover with tape, and set aside for 5 minutes to rest. Using a sharp knife, cut the steak crosswise into 1/8-inch-thick strips.

9.4 BULGOGI (KOREAN BARBECUED BEEF)

Ready in about: 20 minutes - Servings: 6 to 8 - Difficulty: easy

Ingredients:

- 3 ½ tbsp. of soy sauce.
- 5 tbsp. of scallions, chopped on the diagonal.
- 1 ½ tbsp. of toasted crushed sesame seeds.
- 2 tbsp. of sesame oil.
- 1 ½ lb. beef tenderloin or flank steak.

- 1 ½ tbsp. of sugar.
- 1 tsp. of minced garlic.
- 1 large thinly sliced onion.
- 2 tbsp. of rice wine.
- 2 tbsp. of sherry.
- ¼ tsp. of black pepper.

Instructions:

1. Cut the beef into one-and-a-half-inch squares that are 1/8 inches thick. It's easier to thinly dice the beef because it's partially frozen.

2. Combine the beef and the remaining components in a mixing bowl.

3. Over a charcoal fire, grill all of the beef and onion slices until they are just brown on the outside and pink on the inside. It will take 2 to 4 minutes to complete this task.

9.5   PORTERHOUSE WITH SUMMER AU POIVRE SAUCE

Ready in about: 1 hour - Servings: 2 to 3 - Difficulty: hard

Ingredients:

- 2 tbsp. of drained pickled green peppercorns.

- ½ cup of mint leaves.

- Vegetable oil (for the grill).

- ½ cup of basil leaves.

- ½ cup of extra-virgin olive oil.

- 12 lb. porterhouse steak (about 2-inch thick).

- Kosher salt.

Instructions:

1. Prepare a grill for strong indirect heat; spray the grate with vegetable oil. Chop 2 tsp. peppercorns, then basil and mint, coarsely chopped on top of peppercorns. Add the olive oil to a small bowl and season with salt. Set aside a couple more peppercorns, coarsely sliced, for serving.

2. Season the steak with salt and pepper. Grill for 6 to 8 minutes over direct fire, turning steak every 1 minute or 2 to monitor flare-ups and ensure even browning (including standing it on its side with tongs to render and brown fat around edges) until thoroughly browned on all sides (including standing it on its side with tongs to render and brown fat around edges).

3. Grill, turning every 1 to 2 minutes and going closer to or farther away from the heat if required to create even color before an instant-read thermometer inserted into the thickest part of the steak registers 120° F for medium-rare, 10 to 12 minutes (keep tenderloin side away from heat). Allow 15 to 30 minutes to settle on a wire rack spread over a rimmed baking sheet.

4. Cut the meat out from either side of the bone on a cutting board, and slice crosswise. Serve with the sauce and the peppercorns that were saved.

9.6 HASSELBACK SHORT RIB BULGOGI

Ready in about: 40 minutes plus marinating and refrigerating time - Servings: 4 - Difficulty: easy

Ingredients:

For ssamjang:

- ¼ cup of white miso.
- 1 tsp. of sugar.
- 1 tsp. of toasted sesame seeds.
- 1 very finely chopped scallion.
- 1 tsp. of gochujang or the hot chili sauce.
- 1 tsp. of sesame oil.

For scallion salad:

- 2 tsp. of sesame oil.
- 1 tsp. of toasted sesame seeds.
- 6 scallions.
- 2 tsp. of non-seasoned rice vinegar.

For short ribs:

- 2 finely grated garlic cloves.
- 2 tbsp. of unseasoned rice vinegar.
- 1 tbsp. gochugaru or 1 tsp. of crushed red pepper flakes.
- 1 ½ lb. one-inch-thick beef short ribs.
- 1 one-inch piece of finely grated ginger.
- ¼ cup of soy sauce.
- 2 tbsp. of light or dark brown sugar.
- 1 tbsp. toasted sesame oil.
- Vegetable oil.
- Lettuce leaves.
- Kosher salt.

Instructions:

For the ssamjang:

1. In a small cup, combine the scallion, gochujang, miso, sugar, sesame seeds, oil, and 1 tsp. of water.

For scallion's salad:

1. Scallions should be trimmed. Cut crosswise into three-inch lengths, then slice lengthwise into matchsticks as thinly as possible. Drain well, and then pat it dry after rinsing with cold water. Toss the scallions with the vinegar, oil, and sesame seeds in a medium mixing cup.

For short ribs

1. In a medium mixing dish, add the garlic, ginger, soy sauce, brown sugar, vinegar, gochugaru, and sesame oil.

2. Slice short ribs at a steep angle per a quarter-inch with a sharp knife, cutting little more than half-way into the beef. Turn the slicer over and repeat the process, on the other side, keeping the same angle as the first. Toss the meat with the marinade in the bowl, working the marinade through the slashes in the meat. Cover the bowl with a wide plate and set it aside for at least 2 hours or up to 1 day at room temperature.

3. Prepare your grill for medium-high temperature with vegetable oil on the grate. Remove the short ribs from the marinade and season them gently with salt. Grill, rotating every 2 minutes and switch to a cooler section of the grill if necessary, until the meat is solid to the touch and a streak of pink can be seen peeking inside the deepest slashes, 10 minutes.

4. Transfer the short ribs to a chopping board and set aside for at least 5 minutes before chopping through the slashes.

5. Season the scallion salad with salt. Serve the short ribs with ssamjang and scallion salad, if needed, covered in lettuce.

9.7   LACQUERED RIB EYE

Ready in about: 1 hour plus marinating and refrigerating time - Servings: 2 to 4 - Difficulty: hard

Ingredients:

- 2 tbsp. of soy sauce.
- 2 tsp. of sugar.
- Vegetable oil.
- Kosher salt.
- ¼ cup of red wine vinegar or sherry vinegar.
- 1 tbsp. of fish sauce.

- 1 crushed garlic clove.
- Flaky sea salt.
- 2 ½ lb. rib eye.
- Extra-virgin olive oil.
- Lemon wedges.

Instructions:

1. In a shallow saucepan over medium-high heat, bring the soy sauce, vinegar, sugar, fish sauce, and garlic to a simmer. Lower the heat to low and slowly boil for around 7 to 8 minutes, or until the liquid has been decreased by around half. Set aside the sauce.

2. Prepare your grill; spray the grate with oil. Season the steak with pepper and kosher salt. Afterward, grill for around 8 to 9 minutes, rotating every minute over direct heat until thoroughly charred on all sides.

3. Cook the steak over indirect heat, rotating every 2 minutes and shifting closer to or further away from the heat if required to obtain even color, for around 15 minutes, or for the time when a thermometer inserted into the thickest part of the steak shows 100° F. Begin basting the beef. Continue to barbecue, turning and basting with a slight coating of the sauce as required to produce a deep crust on the steak, until its brown and thermometer registers 120° F for medium-rare texture, for about 10 to 12 minutes. Allow 30 minutes for the steak to sit on a wired rack.

4. Break the steak into thick slices on a chopping board. Arrange on a plate and drizzle it with the olive oil before seasoning with. Serve with the wedges of lemon on the side.

9.8   LONDON BROIL II

Ready in about: 45 minutes plus marinating and refrigerating time - Servings: 8 - Difficulty: hard

Ingredients:

- 1 tsp. of salt.

- 1 tbsp. of ketchup.

- ½ tsp. of ground black pepper.

- 4 lb. of flank steak.

- 1 minced clove of garlic.

- 3 tbsp. of soy sauce.

- 1 tbsp. of vegetable oil.

- ½ tsp. of dried oregano.

Instructions:

1. Combine garlic, soy sauce, salt, ketchup, vegetable oil, black pepper, and oregano in a small bowl.

2. Diamond cut all sides of the beef. Both sides of the beef should be rubbed with the garlic mixture. Refrigerate for about 6 hours, or for overnight, wrapped securely in aluminum foil. A few hours, flip the meat.

3. Preheat an outdoor grill to high heat and spray the grate gently with oil.

4. Place the meat on the preheated grill. Cook for about 5 to 7 minutes per side or until cooked to your liking.

9.9   MARINATED FLANK STEAK

Ready in about: 35 minutes plus marinating and refrigerating time - Servings: 6 - Difficulty: hard

Ingredients:

- 1/3 cup of soy sauce.

- 2 tbsp. of fresh lemon juice.

- 1 tbsp. of Dijon mustard.

- ½ cup of vegetable oil.

- ¼ cup of red wine vinegar.

- 1 ½ tbsp. of Worcestershire sauce.

- 2 cloves of garlic, minced.

- 1 ½-lb. of flank steak.

- ½ tsp. of ground black pepper.

Instructions:

1. Combine the soy sauce, oil, vinegar, Worcestershire sauce, lemon juice, garlic, mustard, and ground black pepper in a medium mixing cup. In a shallow glass bowl, put the meat. Apply the marinade over the steak and turn it to cover it fully. Refrigerate for about 6 to 7 hours, sealed.

2. Preheat the grill to medium-high temperature.

3. The grill grate should be oiled. Remove the steaks from the marinade and place them on the grill. Grill the meat for 5 minutes each side or until cooked to your liking.

9.10   KOREAN BBQ SHORT RIBS (GAL-BI)

Ready in about: 7 hours and 25 minutes - Servings: 5 - Difficulty: hard

Ingredients:

- ¾ cup of water.

- ¼ cup of dark brown sugar.

- 1 tbsp. of black pepper.

- ¼ cup of minced garlic.

- 3 lb. Korean-style short ribs.

- ¾ cup of soy sauce.

- 3 tbsp. of white vinegar.

- 2 tbsp. of white sugar.

- 2 tbsp. of sesame oil.

- Half large minced onion.

Instructions:

1. In a big, non-metallic mixing bowl, combine the water, soy sauce, and vinegar. Brown sugar, pepper, white sugar, garlic, sesame oil, and onion can be whisked in before the sugars have dissolved. Cover the ribs with plastic wrap until submerging them in the marinade. Refrigerate for about 12 hours or longer if possible.

2. Preheat the outdoor grill to medium-high.

3. Remove the ribs from the marinade, shake off the residue, and dispose of it. Cook for 7 minutes per side on a preheated grill until the meat is no longer pink.

9.11 GRILLED MEXICAN STEAK

Ready in about: a day - Servings: 6 - Difficulty: hard

Ingredients:

- 5 jalapeno peppers.
- 1 tbsp. of cracked black pepper.
- 1 ½ tsp. of salt.
- ½ cup of cumin seeds.
- 3 cloves of garlic.

- ⅓ cup of fresh lime juice.
- 1 ½ cups of olive oil.
- 1 (3 lb.) skirt or flank steak.
- 2 bunches of cilantro.

Instructions:

1. In a medium sauté pan, over medium-low flame, toast the cumin seeds for about 5 minutes.

2. Combine the jalapenos, garlic, cumin seeds, pepper, lime juice, and salt in a blender. Process it and then pour in the oil and cilantro until smooth.

3. To encourage the marinade to absorb, gently score both sides of the meat with a knife. Place the meat in a big plastic bag or bowl and cover it well with the marinade. Refrigerate for about 1 day or 2 after marinating.

4. Preheat an outdoor grill to high heat and spray the grate gently with oil.

5. Remove the beef from the marinade and toss out the remainder. Sear the meat on high for 1 minute or 2. Reduce the heat to low and cook for an additional 5 minutes per side or until optimal doneness is achieved.

9.12 GRILLED TRI-TIP

Ready in about: 1 hour 50 minutes - Servings: 8 - Difficulty: hard

Ingredients:

- 4 thinly sliced cloves of garlic.

- 4 lb. of tri-tip roast.

- ⅓ cup of salt.

- ⅓ cup of garlic salt.

- ⅓ cup of black pepper.

Instructions:

1. Cut short slits through the top of the roast with a sharp knife. Garlic slices can be stuffed through the slits.

2. Combine the pepper, salt, and garlic salt in a bowl. The whole mixture can be rubbed all over the tri-tip. Refrigerate for at least 1 hour and up to a whole day. Remove the beef from the refrigerator half an hour prior to grilling.

3. Heat an outdoor barbecue to extreme temperatures.

4. To sear the meat and seal in the juices, position it directly over the flame for around 7 to 10 minutes per side.

5. Reduce the heat to medium and roast for another 25 to 30 minutes; careful not to turn the meat too soon. Using a meat thermometer, check for doneness. For medium-rare, the thermometer can register at least 145° F. Enable to rest for 5 minutes before slicing, loosely wrapped with aluminum foil.

9.13 GRILLED HARISSA LAMB CHOPS

Ready in about: 45 minutes - Servings: 4 to 6 - Difficulty: moderate

Ingredients:

- Grill-able vegetables of your choice.

- 2 to 3 lbs. lamb chops, lamb loin chops, or sirloin steaks.

- Zucchini, bell pepper, summer squash, onion, mushrooms, eggplant, etc.

- 2 handfuls of fresh leaves of mint.

- Olive oil.

For Harissa spice rub:

- 1 tbsp. of coriander.

- 1 tbsp. of granulated garlic.

- 1 tbsp. of cumin.

- 1 tbsp. of smoked paprika.

- 2 tsp. of salt.

- 1 tsp. of caraway seeds.

- 1 tsp. of dried mint.

For Harissa yogurt:

- 1 tbsp. of harissa paste.

- Serve with Grilled Vegetables and your choice of grain, basmati rice, quinoa, or couscous.

- 1 cup of plain, full-fat Greek yogurt.

- 1 tsp. of smoked paprika.

For garnish:

- A couple of fresh mint leaves or parsley leaves.

Instructions:

1. Preheat the oven. Preheat the grill to medium-high.

2. Lamb chops can be sliced into single portions. Allow it to dry.

3. In a small dish, combine together the salt and spices.

4. Dip all sides of every chop, including the fatty tip, in the prepared rub, then tap off the excess and put on a sheet pan.

5. If you're grilling vegetables, toss them gently with salt, olive oil, and pepper and cook them first. Cover and put aside before ready to serve.

6. The lamb chops can be grilled. Using an olive oil spray, cover the grill. Place the chops on the grill and cook for around 3 to 4 minutes or until they have developed strong grill marks.

7. Switch the lamb chops over after spraying them with olive oil. Reduce the heat to medium and cook for another 4 to 5 minutes. Then, lean the fatty side of the lamb chops against each other on the grill until they're sitting straight. Cover and simmer for another couple of minutes or until the fatty coating has melted away. Remove the grill pan from the fire and cover with foil before serving.

8. Start with a small amount of yogurt and harissa paste, then apply more to taste.

9. Break the grilled vegetables into eatable bites and arrange them on a platter to eat. Add the grilled chops on top. Serve with mint leaves as a garnish.

10. Serve the prepared yogurt on the side or drizzle some over each chop.

9.14 GRILLED LAMB KEBABS WITH HERB SALAD AND YOGURT SAUCE

Ready in about: 40 minutes - Servings: 3 - Difficulty: moderate

Ingredients:

For lamb kababs:

- Half finely diced onion.
- 2 tsp. of cumin.
- 2 tsp. of sumac.
- 1 ½ tsp. of kosher salt.
- 1 lb. ground lamb.
- 3 garlic cloves, finely minced.
- 2 tsp. of coriander.
- 1 tsp. of Aleppo Chili flakes.
- 2 tbsp. of chopped mint.
- 12 x 12-inch overnight soaked wood skewers.

For yogurt sauce:

- 2 tbsp. of freshly chopped dill.
- 1 cup of plain Greek yogurt.
- 2 finely minced garlic cloves.
- ¼ tsp. of salt.

For herb salad:

- 1 cup of fresh herbs (any mix of Italian parsley, dill, mint, cilantro).
- 1 Turkish cucumber, thinly sliced.
- 1 green onion thinly sliced.
- 2 to 3 handfuls of baby spring greens.
- 1 cup of sprouts—sunflower, radish, or baby pea shoots.
- 2 thinly sliced radishes.

For dressing:

- Lemon zest.
- ¼ tsp. of salt.
- ½ tsp. of sumac.
- 2 tbsp. of olive oil.
- 2 tbsp. of lemon juice.
- ¼ tsp. of cracked pepper.

Instructions:

1. Start the grill by soaking the skewers.

2. Mix the ingredients of the lamb in a bowl and put it aside.

3. In a shallow bowl, combine the ingredients for the yogurt sauce.

4. Place the ingredients of the salad in a medium-sized bowl after they've been prepped. In a shallow mixing cup, combine the ingredients of salad dressing.

5. Assemble the kebabs. Divide the meat into 6 equal-sized pieces with wet paws, around half a cup total. Form one into a large oval form with 2 skewers, then begin forming and stretch it until the meat is around 4 to 5 inches long and one and a half inches in its diameter. Use a rolling pin to softly roll up the meat on the soaked skewers and make it smooth, and even so, they don't have to be flawless. To keep the lamb on the skewers, make sure they are balanced down the center.

6. To avoid sticking, spray, brush or roll the chicken in olive oil and grill it over medium-high flame, rotating every couple of minutes. Instead of picking up the lamb by the skewers, use tongs to flip it. This would help the lamb remain on the skewers. Turn off the grill and cover it after the lamb has been seared on both sides, enabling the lamb to rest within a couple of minutes as you cook the dishes.

7. Toss together the salad with a dollop of yogurt-dill sauce on one side of the platter. Using 2 to 3 skewers, adorn the sauce. Place the salad on the other side of the plate and serve right away.

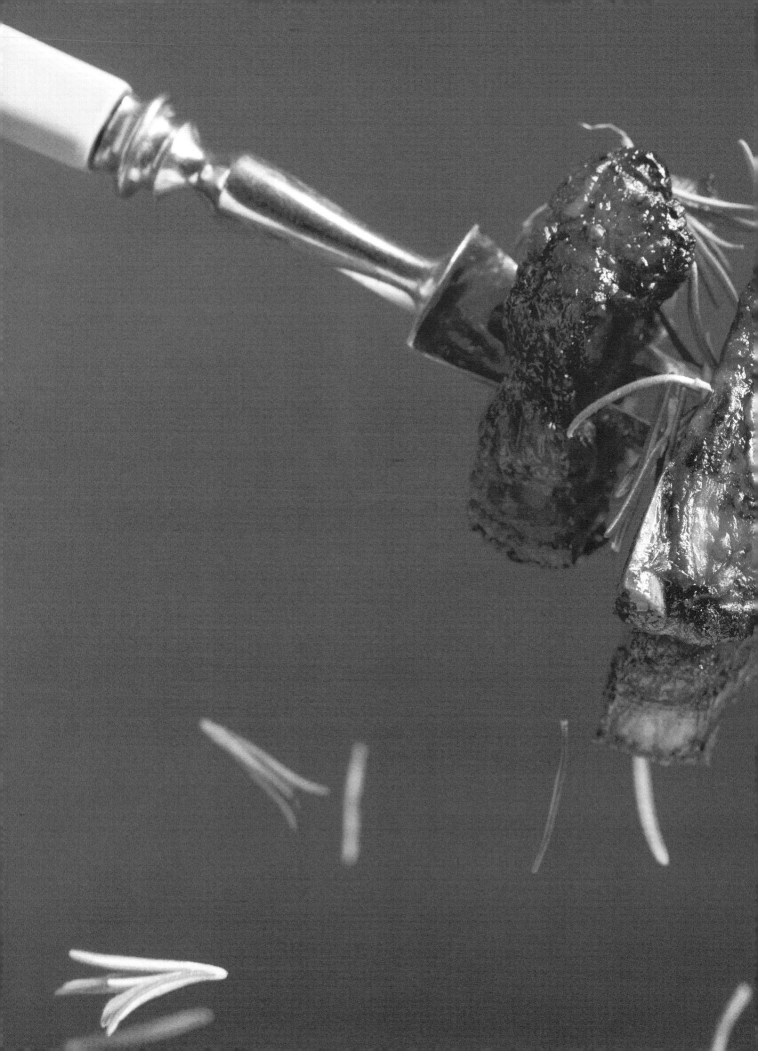

CHAPTER
10

PORK
RECIPES

CHAPTER 10 - PORK RECIPES

10.1 GRILLED PORK CHOPS WITH FRIED SAGE LEAVES

Ready in about: 10 minutes - Servings: 4 - Difficulty: easy

Ingredients:

- Juice of 1 lemon.

- 2 tbsp. of olive oil.

- About ½ cup vegetable oil (enough for half an inch in the pan).

- 4 loin pork chops.

- 1 minced clove of garlic.

- Coarse salt and freshly ground pepper to taste.

- 30 fresh sage leaves.

Instructions:

1. Combine garlic, lemon juice, and olive oil in a bowl and coat pork chops. Enable 30 minutes to marinate at room temperature. Season with pepper and salt and grill for around 20 minutes or until cooked through, rotating once over hot coals.

2. Heat the vegetable oil in a skillet and fry the sage leaves for around 2 minutes, or until crisp. Drain on paper towels after removing using a slotted spoon.

3. Serve pork chops with sage leaves as a garnish.

10.2 NORTH CAROLINA-STYLE PULLED PORK

Ready in about: 5 to 7 hours - Servings: 10 to 12 - Difficulty: hard

Ingredients:

For pork:

- ¼ cup of basic rub for barbecue.

- 1 bone-in pork shoulder roast (5 to 6 lb.).

- 4 cups of hickory chips, soaked in cold water for 1 hour and then drained.

For the vinegar sauce:

- 2 tbsp. of sugar, or to taste.

- 1 ½ cups of cider vinegar.

- 1 tbsp. of red pepper flakes.

- ½ tsp. of freshly ground black pepper.

- 2 tsp. of salt, or to taste.

Instructions:

1. Preheat the grill to 325° F. If using wood, create a fire on opposite sides of the grill; if using gas, build a fire on one side or opposite sides of the grill. Rub the rub all over the bacon.

2. While utilizing charcoal, apply fresh coals and half cup wood chips to each mound of coals every hour for the first 4 hours. Place wood chips in the smoker box if using coal, and preheat before smoke appears.

3. Place the pork fat side up on the barbecue, away from the flames, over the drip tray. Grill for 4 to 6 hours, or until the beef is nicely browned and cooked through, or until the internal temperature reaches 195° F.

4. Meanwhile, whisk together the ingredients for the vinegar sauce in a bowl of 3/4 cup sugar. If required, season with more salt or sugar to taste.

5. Transfer the fried pork to a cutting board, cover with tape, and set aside for 15 minutes or until cool enough to touch. Remove all flesh, bones, or fat from the meat and discard. Pull each slice of pork into shreds about 2 inches long by 14 inches wide with your fingertips or a fork. (Alternatively, use a cleaver to finely cut the meat.) Pour 1 cup vinegar sauce, or sufficiently to hold the meat moist and juicy, into a metal or foil jar. Cover with foil and remain warm on the barbecue before ready to eat. Serve with coleslaw and the leftover sauce on the hamburger buns.

10.3 GRILLED PORK PORTERHOUSE WITH AN APPLE-MAPLE-GINGER SAUCE

Ready in about: 30 minutes plus refrigeration - Servings: 6 - Difficulty: hard

Ingredients:

For the brine:

- 5 tbsp. of kosher salt.
- 3 tbsp. of crushed garlic.
- ¾ cup onion slices, cut into ¼-inch-thick rings.
- ¼ cup of maple syrup.
- 3 tbsp. of sliced peeled fresh ginger.
- 1 sprig of fresh sage.
- 5 bay leaves.
- 6 (1 ¼-inch-thick) pork loin chops.
- 2 tsp. of peppercorns.

For the infused oil:

- 1 bay leaf.
- 2 tbsp. of minced shallot.
- 1 tbsp. of coriander seeds.
- 1 tbsp. of peppercorns.
- 1 tsp. of minced fresh thyme.
- ½ cup of vegetable oil.
- 1 tsp. of minced fresh rosemary.

For the sauce:

- ¼ cup of minced shallot.
- 2 cups of apple juice.
- Three-star anise.
- ½ cup of maple syrup.
- 2 tbsp. of butter.
- 1 tbsp. of minced garlic.
- ½ cup of chicken stock.
- 2 tbsp. of minced fresh ginger.
- ½ vanilla bean, seeds scraped.
- Salt and freshly ground black pepper to taste.
- 1 tbsp. of agar.

Instructions:

1. Stir all of the brine ingredients except pork into 1-quart water in a big pot and bring to a boil 24 hours before cooking. Allow cooling to room temperature before serving. Refrigerate pork chops after submerging them in brine.

2. Prepare the flavored oil the next morning by grinding bay leaf, coriander, and peppercorns in a spice mill or a clean coffee grinder, then mixing with the remaining ingredients in a medium cup. Enable to cool to room temperature.

3. To make the sauce, first, melt butter in a saucepan over a medium-low flame. Add the shallot and cook for 4 minutes, or until caramelized. Cook for 1 minute after adding the garlic. Apple juice, star anise, chicken stock, and ginger are applied to the pot. Bring to a boil, then limit to ¼ of its original volume. Simmer for 3 minutes with vanilla pod maple syrup, and seeds, and agar.

4. Remove the pan from the sun. Drop the vanilla pod and star anise. In a blender or food processor, puree the paste, then strain it into a jar via a fine-mesh sieve. Season with salt and pepper to taste.

5. Heat a charcoal or gas grill to medium-high temperatures. Clean the meat by rinsing it and patting it dry with paper towels; after brushing the chops with the flavored oil, season gently with salt. Grill to medium doneness, around 6 minutes per foot, or until internal temperature hits 135° F to 140° F on a thermometer and center is light pink. Allow for a 5-minute rest before serving. Serve with a warm sauce drizzled on top.

10.4 BBQ PORK TENDERLOIN

Ready in about: 1 hour and 40 minutes plus marinating and refrigerating time - Servings: 4 to 6 - Difficulty: hard

Ingredients:

- 2 cups of chopped onions.
- ½ cup of soy sauce.
- ¼ cup of sugar.
- 4 minced cloves of garlic.
- ½ cup of fresh lemon juice.

- ½ cup of corn oil.
- 3 to 4 tbsp. of ground coriander.
- 6 pork tenderloins.
- Tabasco sauce.

Instructions:

1. Stir together lemon juice, garlic, onions, oil, soy sauce, coriander, sugar, and Tabasco sauce in a large mixing cup.

2. Place entire tenderloins in the marinade and then set them aside in the refrigerator for around 5 to 6 hours.

3. Set the grill about 5 inches above the heat.

4. Remove the meat from the marinade, transfer the marinade to a frying pan and keep it warm as the meat heats.

5. Place tenderloins on the grill, leaving enough room between them to spin. Turn the parts after around 30 minutes and spoon the marinade over them; repeat on the other side. Grill for about 1 hour.

6. Spread cooked marinade over each tenderloin before eating.

10.5 GRILLED PORK LOIN WITH WINE-SALT RUB

Ready in about: 2 hours 30 minutes plus marinating time - Servings: 8 to 10 - Difficulty: hard

Ingredients:

- ¾ cup of coarse sea salt.

- 2 strips of finely chopped lemon zest.

- 1 (about 3 ½-lb.) boneless pork loin.

- 2 cups of fruity white wine, such as riesling or gewürztraminer.

- 8 sprigs of fresh thyme leaves stripped (about 2 tbsp. of leaves).

- 1 cup of sugar.

Instructions:

1. Reduce wine by half in a medium heavy-bottomed pan over medium heat for 30 minutes; reduce heat to low and proceed to cook down to 2 tsp. Enable to cool absolutely.

2. Combine the salt, lemon zest, thyme leaves, and wine reduction in a food processor. Process 2 or 3 times. Add the sugar and pulse once more before the mixture resembles moist powder. If the mixture is stickier, spread it out uniformly on a sheet pan and set it aside for some hours or for overnight.

3. Put the pork in a baking tray. Using a half cup of salt rub, rub the pork all over. Refrigerate for at least 3 to 4 hours or for overnight, securely wrapped in plastic wrap.

4. Light your grill for indirect high-heat cooking by stacking charcoal on 1 side and keeping the other unlit. To collect some drips, put a piece of foil or a disposable metal roasting pan below the grill on the unlit side. Place the pork over the foil on the barbecue. Cover the grill and cook for 1 hour to 90 minutes, turn it every 30 minutes until meat hits 140° F in the middle. Allow 10 minutes to rest before slicing it.

10.6 GRILLED PORK SHOULDER STEAKS WITH HERB SALAD

Ready in about: 40 minutes plus marinating time - Servings: 8 - Difficulty: hard

Ingredients:

- 6 garlic cloves.

- ⅓ cup plus 3 tbsp. of fresh lime juice.

- 8 ¾-inch thick pork shoulder steaks.

- 3 cups of Thai or sweet basil leaves, Dill or cilantro leaves.

- 4 medium shallots.

- ⅓ cup plus 3 tbsp. of fish sauce.

- 3 tbsp. of light brown sugar.

- 2 thinly sliced red or green Thai chilies.

- A pinch of salt and pepper.

Instructions:

1. In a mixer, combine minced shallots, garlic, ⅓ cup of fish sauce, ⅓ cup of lime juice, and 2 tsp. brown sugar until creamy.

2. Season steaks with a pinch of salt and pepper. Place in a big mixing bowl or a 12x9 inches baking dish to cool. Pour the marinade over the steaks and transform them with tongs to cover them properly. Allow to stay for 1 hour at room temperature, or cover and chill for up to 12 hours, turning once (halfway through if you can).

3. Preheat your grill to high. 7 to 9 minutes on the grill, rotating steaks every minute or 2 until gently charred and crisp, and an instant-read thermometer inserted into the thickest portion registers 140° F. Place the steaks on a cutting board and set aside for at least 5 minutes before slicing thinly.

4. In a big mixing bowl, combine the chilies, the remaining 3 tbsp. of fish sauce, the remaining 3 tbsp. of lime juice, the remaining 1 tbsp. of brown sugar, and 1tbsp. of water. Toss in the cut shallots and spices, seasoning gently with salt.

5. Arrange the sliced meat on a platter and top it with the herb salad.

10.7 SPICY PORK SKEWERS

Ready in about: 40 minutes plus marinating time - Servings: 8 - Difficulty: hard

Ingredients:

- Half small red onion, thinly sliced.

- 8 garlic cloves, coarsely chopped.

- ½ cup of soy sauce.

- ¼ cup of sugar.

- 1 tbsp. of kosher salt, plus more.

- 2 lb. skinless, boneless pork shoulder.

- 12 red Thai chilies, coarsely chopped.

- 1 cup of Sprite or 7UP.

- ⅓ cup cane vinegar (such as Datu Puti) or unseasoned rice vinegar.

- 1 tbsp. of black peppercorns.

- 6 dried shiitake mushrooms.

Instructions:

1. Freeze pork on a rimmed baking sheet for 45 to 60 minutes or until really solid around the edges. Take the pork from the fridge and thinly slice it. Using a sharp knife, break the bits lengthwise into 1"–2" short strips.

2. In a big resealable plastic container, add the onion, garlic, chilies, Sprite, vinegar, sugar, soy sauce, peppercorns, and 1 tsp. salt. Mushrooms, ground to a powder in a spice mill or mortar and pestle, are whisked onto the marinade. Apply a few bits of pork at a time, covering thoroughly so they don't cling together and can consume the marinade equally. Chill for 6 to 8 hours, covered.

3. Preheat the grill to medium-high. Remove the pork from the marinade and skewer it. Bring the marinade to a boil in a shallow saucepan over high heat on the barbecue. Cook for 1 minute, skimming any foam that grows to the tip. Transfer to a cooler portion of the barbecue.

4. Season pork lightly with salt and roast, uncovered, for 2 minutes or until well browned. Switch the beef over and baste with the marinade. Continue to barbecue, rotating and basting every minute, for another 4 minutes or until the chicken is cooked through and browned all over.

10.8 BARBECUE PORK WITH BLISTERED CHILE—PUMPKIN SEED SALSA

Ready in about: 40 minutes plus marinating time - Servings: 4 - Difficulty: hard

Ingredients:

For salsa:

- 2 jalapeños.
- ¼ cup of finely chopped roasted pumpkin seeds.
- ¼ large white onion.
- ¼ cup of chopped cilantro.
- ¼ cup of olive oil.
- Kosher salt.
- 3 tbsp. of lime juice.

For pork:

- 2 tbsp. of light brown sugar.
- 2 tbsp. of paprika.
- 1 tsp. of freshly ground black pepper.
- 1 ¼ lb. of boneless pork shoulder.
- 2 tbsp. of mustard powder.
- 2 tsp. of garlic powder.
- ½ tsp. of cayenne pepper.
- Kosher salt.
- Vegetable oil.

Instructions:

For salsa:

1. Over a gas burner, cook onion and jalapeños, regularly rotating, until they are charred and softening, around 4 minutes. Allow cooling. Chop the onion finely. Remove the seeds from the chilies and cut them finely. In a shallow bowl, combine the onion, cilantro, chilies, oil, pumpkin seeds, and lime juice. Season with salt.

2. Salsa may be prepared up to a day ahead of time. Cover and set aside to relax.

For pork:

1. Freeze pork for 20 to 30 minutes, or until really firm at the edges. If required, cut it crosswise into 1 1/2"–2" strips after slicing 1/4" wide. Refrigerate before able to barbecue.

2. Brown sugar, paprika, mustard powder, black pepper, garlic powder, and salt are combined in a bowl.

3. Prepare a grill for indirect medium-high fire. Oil the grates. Pork should be threaded onto the skewers, folded, and piled on top of each other to create a compact shape. Season it with salt and then coat with the brown sugar mixture in multiple passes, taking some minutes for each to enable the rub to stick. Grill for around 4 minutes over direct fire, turning every minute or so until it is browned and starting to char in spots. Continue to barbecue on the cool side of the grill for another 5 minutes or until it is cooked. Serve the pork with salsa on top.

10.9 CHAR SIU (CHINESE BBQ PORK)

Ready in about: 3 hours and 40 minutes - Servings: 4 - Difficulty: hard

Ingredients:

- ½ cup of soy sauce.

- ⅓ cup of ketchup.

- ¼ cup of Chinese rice wine.

- 2 pork tenderloins.

- ⅓ cup of honey.

- ⅓ cup of brown sugar.

- 2 tbsp. of hoisin sauce.

- 1 tsp. of Chinese five-spice powder.

Instructions:

1. Break pork into 1 ½ to two-inch-long strips against the grain and position in a wide resealable plastic container.

2. In a saucepan over medium-low heat, add soy sauce, ketchup, honey, brown sugar, hoisin sauce, rice wine, and the Chinese five-spice powder. For around 2 to 3 minutes, cook and stir until just mixed and slightly wet. Cover the bag with the pork and the marinade, force out the air and close it. Turn the bag a couple of times to ensure that all of the pork bits are covered in the marinade.

3. Refrigerate the pork for about 2 to 3 hours or for overnight.

4. Preheat your grill to medium-high temperature and spray the grate gently with oil.

5. Take the pork from the marinade and shake it to get rid of the extra liquid. Remove and discard any leftover marinade.

6. Cook the pork for about 30 minutes on a preheated grill. Place a small cup of water on the grill and proceed to cook, rotating the pork periodically, for around 1 hour, or until it is cooked through. At least 145° F should be read on a thermometer placed into the middle.

10.10   CHEF JOHN'S YUCATAN-STYLE GRILLED PORK

Ready in about: 4 hours and 23 minutes - Servings: 6 - Difficulty: hard

Ingredients:

- 2 lemons, juiced, or more to taste.
- 6 cloves of garlic, minced.
- 1 tsp. of annatto powder, or more to taste, plus more to sprinkle on before grilling.
- 1 tsp. of ground cumin.
- ½ tsp. of dried oregano.
- 2 oranges, juiced.

- 2 limes, juiced, or more to taste.
- 1 tbsp. of kosher salt.
- 1 tsp. of ground dried chipotle pepper.
- ½ tsp. of cayenne pepper.
- ½ tsp. of freshly ground black pepper.
- 1 tbsp. of vegetable oil.
- 2 pork tenderloins, trimmed.

Instructions:

1. In a mixing bowl, combine the lemon juice, orange juice, and lime juice. Garlic, annatto powder, kosher salt, chipotle powder, cayenne, oregano, ground cumin, and black pepper are also good additions. Whisk before it is well combined.

2. Break the tenderloins crosswise in half, then lengthwise in half. Place the bits in the marinade and cover them fully. Cover the meat and marinade in plastic wrap, with the wrap reaching the surface. (Alternatively, place the mixture in a resealable plastic bag.) Refrigerate for 4 to 6 hours before serving.

3. Remove the pork from the marinade and put it in a paper towel-lined bowl to absorb the excess moisture. Paper towels can be discarded. Drizzle the pork with vegetable oil and a pinch of annatto powder.

4. Preheat an outdoor grill to medium-high heat and spray the grate gently with oil.

5. On a hot grill, equally, space the bits. Allow meat to sear on the grate for 4 to 5 minutes. Grill for another 4 or 5 minutes, on the other side. A thermometer inserted in the middle should read 135 to 140° F. Transfer the meat to a serving platter and set aside for 5 minutes before serving.

10.11 GRILLED MONGOLIAN PORK CHOPS

Ready in about: 7 hours - Servings: 2 - Difficulty: hard

Ingredients:

- 4 cloves of garlic, minced.
- 1 tbsp. of grated fresh ginger.
- 1 tbsp. of rice vinegar.
- 2 tsp. of sesame oil.
- 1 ½ tsp. of hot sauce.
- ½ tsp. of freshly ground black pepper.
- ¼ cup of red wine vinegar.
- 2 tbsp. of hot mustard powder or Chinese style.
- ⅓ cup of creme fraiche.
- ½ cup of hoisin sauce.

- 1 ½ tbsp. of soy sauce.
- 1 tbsp. of red wine vinegar.
- 1 tbsp. of sherry vinegar.
- 2 tsp. of white sugar.
- ½ tsp. of ground white pepper.
- 2 (around 10 oz.) thick pork chops.
- 3 tbsp. of white sugar.
- 1 egg yolk.
- 1 tsp. of Dijon mustard.
- Cayenne pepper to taste.
- ¼ tsp. of ground turmeric.

Instructions:

1. In a large mixing cup, add hoisin sauce, soy sauce, garlic, ginger, 1 tbsp. red wine vinegar, sherry vinegar, rice vinegar, sesame oil, 2 tsp. sugar, white pepper, hot sauce, and black pepper. Set aside after vigorously whisking.

2. Put pork chops in a resealable freezer bag and spill slightly more than half of the marinade over them. Refrigerate for 6 to 8 hours after sealing the container. Save the remainder of the marinade.

3. In a shallow saucepan over medium-low heat, combine ¼ cup of red wine vinegar, 2 tbsp. hot mustard powder, 3 tbsp. sugar, and egg yolk. Remove from heat after 5 minutes of whisking until slightly thickened.

4. Combine the creme fraiche, turmeric, Dijon mustard, and cayenne pepper in a large mixing dish. Refrigerate until ready to use.

5. Take the pork chops out of the marinade and wipe them dry with a paper towel.

6. Preheat an outdoor grill to high heat and brush the grate gently with oil.

7. On a preheated grill, cook pork chops until browned grill marks emerge on both sides, around 4 minutes per side.

8. Remove the pork chops from the immediate heat source. Cook, coating each side with the remaining marinade until no longer pink within, around 30 minutes over indirect medium heat. The temperature can read 145° F on a thermometer inserted into the middle. Serve pork chops with mustard sauce on top.

10.12   HONEY-GRILLED PORK CHOPS

Ready in about: 5 hours 35 minutes - Servings: 6 - Difficulty: hard

Ingredients:

- 6 tbsp. of soy sauce.

- ½ cup of honey.

- 3 tbsp. of lemon juice.

- 6 pork chops.

- 2 tsp. of minced garlic.

Instructions:

1. In a cup, whisk together the soy sauce, lemon juice, honey, and garlic until the marinade is smooth. Pour the marinade into a resealable plastic container, reserving ¼ cup for basting in a bowl. Place the pork chops in the container, cover with the marinade, force out any extra air, and close the bag; marinate for at least 5 to 6 hours in the refrigerator.

2. Preheat the grill to medium heat and brush the grate gently with oil. Shake off the leftover marinade from the pork chops. Remove and discard any leftover marinade.

3. Pork chops should be cooked through after 20 minutes on a preheated grill, basting with the reserved marinade throughout the last few minutes. The temperature can read 145° F on the thermometer inserted into the middle. Allow 3 minutes for the pork chops to rest before chopping and eating.

10.13   GRILLED PORK LOIN WITH APPLE, SERRANO, HARD CIDER SAGE CREAM

Ready in about: 1 hour plus marinating time - Servings: 4 - Difficulty: moderate

Ingredients:

For pork:

- ¼ cup of fresh lime juice and zest from 1 lime.
- ¼ cup of maple syrup.
- 1 ½ tsp. of kosher salt.
- 1 ½ lb. of pork tenderloin whole.
- ¼ cup of fresh orange juice and zest from 1 orange.
- 3 garlic cloves minced.

For hard cider sauce:

- 1 large shallot finely diced.
- ½ cup of chicken stock.
- 3/4 cup of heavy whipping cream.
- Salt to taste.
- 1 tbsp. of butter.
- 1 cup of hard apple cider.
- ½ of the whole serrano chili, seeded and finely diced.
- Freshly ground black pepper.

For apples:

- 1 tbsp. of olive oil.
- 1 tbsp. of fresh chopped sage.
- 1 tbsp. of butter.
- 3 apples unpeeled and thickly sliced.
- 1 ½ tsp. of sugar.
- Splash cider.
- ¼ tsp. of salt.

Instructions:

- Marinate pork for at least 2 hours and up to 24 hours by mixing the first 6 ingredients in a sealable container, refrigerating, and enabling it to marinate for at least 2 hours and up to 24 hours. The more time you get, the stronger. Before grilling, get to room temperature. To make the hard cider sauce, combine all of the ingredients in a mixing bowl. Sauté shallots in butter in a medium pot until soft. Bring the cider, chicken stock, and serrano chili to a boil, then reduce to low heat and cook, uncovered, for 20 minutes, or until the liquid has decreased by half. Heavy whipped cream should be added at this stage. Continue to cook, stirring regularly, until the sauce thickens and becomes a lovely pale golden color, around 15 minutes more. To taste, season with salt and cracked pepper.

- Sauté apples in butter and olive oil in a heavy bottom skillet over medium heat until golden and tender. Season with sage, salt, and sugar, as well as a splash of cider. Switch off the fire and put the cider aside until it has evaporated.

- Pork loin should be grilled on medium fire, regularly rotating until both sides are seared (about 12 minutes). Reduce the heat to low and cook. Remove the pork from the heat as soon as the internal temperature reaches 140° F. Seal tightly in foil, and set aside for 10 minutes before slicing.

- Place the apple mixture over and around the pork slices, which should be one-inch thick. Garnish with sage leaves. Pour the hard cider sauce on top.

10.14 GRILLED PORK TENDERLOIN WITH STRAWBERRIES AND ROSEMARY

Ready in about: 1 hour plus marinating time - Servings: 4 - Difficulty: moderate

Ingredients:

- 1 lb. pork tenderloin.

For marinade:

- ¼ cup of olive oil.
- 1 tsp. of pepper.
- 3 garlic cloves.

- ¼ cup of balsamic vinegar.
- 1 ½ tsp. of salt.
- 2 tsp. of fresh rosemary.

Savory strawberry compote:

- 1 finely chopped small shallot.
- ½ cup of white wine.
- 1 tbsp. of olive oil.
- 2 cups of strawberries, small diced.

- 2 tbsp. of sugar.
- 1 tsp. of lemon juice.
- A generous pinch of salt and pepper.

For garnish:

- 1 cup of diced strawberries, glaze, fresh rosemary sprigs.

Instructions.

1. In a mixer, combine both of the marinade components. Coat both sides of the loin with the marinade in a big Ziploc bag or a small baking dish. Let it be in the refrigerator for 1 hour or overnight.

2. Heat the oil in a small pot over medium-low heat, then add the shallot. Stir and simmer for 2 to 3 minutes, or until golden. Add the wine, strawberries, sugar, salt, and pepper to taste. Take to a low boil, then reduce to low heat. Cook, stirring regularly until the wine has diminished and the strawberries have thickened around 10 minutes. It should seem as though there is a loose jam. Add a squeeze of lemon to the mix. Then set aside.

3. Preheat the grill to high.

4. Remove the loin from the marinade and set aside any leftover marinade in a small jar. Boil for 1 minute, or until it has darkened—you'll baste the loin with this fried marinade when it's on the grill.

5. Scrape the grill clean until it's hot. Turn the grill to medium-high and cook the pork loin for 12 minutes overall, turning and basting every 3 minutes. Between turns, cover. Make sure the temperature is right. Continue to cook on the grill, lowering the heat if possible (or finish in the oven) until the loin hits 140° F at its thickest stage. Allow 5 to 10 minutes for resting.

6. When ready to eat, slice the loin into ¾-inch slices and put it on a plate with the compote on top (or place pork over the compote).

7. Use rosemary sprigs, fresh diced strawberry, and the balsamic reduction for garnish.

CHAPTER 11

SEAFOOD RECIPES

CHAPTER 11 - SEAFOOD RECIPES

11.1 CHARCOAL-GRILLED STRIPED BASS

Ready in about: 45 minutes - Servings: 4 to 8 - Difficulty: moderate

Ingredients:

- Salt and freshly ground black pepper.

- 1 large sprig of fresh rosemary.

- Oil.

- 1 (3-to 4-lb.) striped bass, gutted.

- 1 peeled clove of garlic.

- 1 bay leaf.

- ¼-lb. of (1 stick) butter, melted and kept hot.

- Lemon wedges.

- ¼ cup of chopped fresh parsley.

Instructions:

1. Construct a charcoal fire. They're ready as white ash forms on top of the coals.

2. Prepare the fish in the meantime. Salt and pepper, it both inside and out. Using a knife, shave a garlic clove into slivers. Create a few small incisions around the backbone of the fish using a thin paring knife. Garlic slivers can be included.

3. In the cavity of the fish, place a rosemary sprig and a bay leaf. To protect the cavity, tie the fish in 2 or 3 positions with thread. Using a generous quantity of oil, massage the fish all over. Put the fish on a hot grill and cook for 10 to 15 minutes; brush with butter if desired.

4. Remove the fish from the grill with a pancake turner, spatula, or both and flip it. Cook for a further 10 to 15 minutes on that side, or until the fish is cooked through and the meat flakes easily when examined with a fork. Cooking time is defined by the size of the fish, the temperature of the heat, and the proximity of the fish to the coals.

5. Place the fish on a hot platter and drizzle with the remaining butter. Add parsley and lemon wedges for a finishing touch.

11.2 WHITE FISH FILLETS WITH GRILLED CABBAGE

Ready in about: 45 minutes - Servings: 2 to 4 - Difficulty: moderate

Ingredients:

- 4 savoy cabbage leaves.

- 4 tsp. of chopped fresh dill.

- Olive oil as needed.

- 2 tbsp. of butter.

- 1 meaty skeleton from a small white fish, like sea bass, chopped.

- Microgreens or flowers for garnish.

- Salt for cabbage.

- 8 oz. of skinless white-fish fillets, cut into 4 small pieces.

- Salt and black pepper as per your taste.

- 1 tbsp. of neutral oil (like grapeseed or corn).

- Several sprigs of fresh thyme.

- 2 cups dry white wine.

Instructions:

1. Heat a grill with the rack next to the flame, and really nice.

2. Bring a big pot of salted water to a boil. Remove the thickest section of each cabbage leaf's central vein without slicing the leaf in half. Blanch cabbage leaves in boiling water for 30 seconds or until only tender; drain on paper towels. Place a slice of fish on one side of each leaf and top with 1 tsp. dill, salt and pepper, and a drizzle of olive oil. To make an oval, fold the other half of the leaf over the fish and trim the edges with a large cookie cutter or a knife. Apply a small amount of olive oil to the exterior.

3. In a skillet wide enough to keep fish bones in one layer, heat neutral oil and 1 tbsp. butter over medium-high heat; when the butter melts, add thyme and fish bones and fry, stirring periodically, until very well browned around 5 minutes. Cook, sometimes stirring, until the remaining 1 tbsp. of butter has melted and the wine has decreased in amount, around 10 minutes. Remove the bones from the fish and discard them. Season the sauce with salt and pepper and hold it warm as you cook the fish.

4. Grill the fish packets for 30 seconds on either side; the cabbage should brown, and the fish should scarcely steam.

5. To foam up the sauce, whisk it or use an immersion blender. Serve by drizzling sauce over cabbage and fish and garnishing with microgreens or flowers.

11.3   GRILLED SWORDFISH STEAKS WITH ORANGE THYME SAUCE

Ready in about: 30 minutes - Servings: 4 - Difficulty: moderate

Ingredients:

- 3 tbsp. of olive oil.

- 1 minced shallot.

- 2 medium-ripe tomatoes, chopped.

- 2/3 cup of fresh orange juice.

- Salt and ground pepper according to taste.

- 2 swordfish steaks (about 2 to 2 ½ lb. in all).

- 2 tbsp. of unsalted butter.

- 1 minced clove of garlic.

- ¼ cup of fresh thyme leaves.

- ¼ cup to half cup dry white wine.

Instructions:

1. Using paper towels rinse swordfish steaks. Using 2 tsp. of olive oil, coat all sides of the chicken.

2. In a pan with 1 tbsp. of butter, heat the remaining 1 tbsp. of olive oil. Cook until the garlic and shallots are tender. Cook for 3 minutes after adding the thyme and tomatoes.

3. Cook for 5 minutes more after adding the white wine and orange juice. Season the fish with pepper and salt and put aside until ready to cook.

4. Preheat the grill. Cook for 5 minutes on either side. In the meantime, put the sauce to a boil. Remove the pan from the heat and whisk the leftover 1 tbsp. of butter. Serve the steaks with the sauce.

11.4 STEPHAN PYLES'S GRILLED REDFISH WITH SMOKED TOMATO SALSA AND BLACK-EYED PEAS–JICAMA RELISH

Ready in about: 10 minutes - Servings: 4 - Difficulty: easy

Ingredients:

For the black-eyed pea–jicama relish:

- 1 ½ cups of fish or chicken stock.

- 1 tbsp. of each diced red and yellow bell pepper.

- 1 small serrano chili, seeded and minced.

- 3 tbsp. of diced mango, papaya, or cantaloupe.

- Salt to taste.

- 6 tbsp. of dried black-eyed peas.

- 2 oz. of jicama, peeled and cut into small, ¼-inch pieces.

- 1 tbsp. of diced sweet onion.

- 2 tbsp. of diced cucumber.

- 1 tsp. of finely chopped fresh spearmint.

For the smoked tomato salsa:

- 1 tbsp. of extra virgin olive oil.

- 3 medium-size scallions, including white and green parts, diced.

- ½ cup fresh cilantro leaves, finely chopped.

- Salt and freshly ground black pepper to taste.

- 4 small (about 1 lb.) very ripe tomatoes.

- 2 tbsp. of each diced green, red and yellow bell pepper.

- 3 small serrano chilies, seeded and diced.

- Salt and freshly ground black pepper to taste.

- 4 (6-oz.) redfish fillets.

- 2 tbsp. of tasteless vegetable oil or clarified butter.

Instructions:

1. 1 hour before serving, render the black-eyed pea relish. Soak black-eyed peas in warm water for 20 to 30 minutes, or until they are soft and have grown marginally in bulk. Bring them to a boil in fish or chicken stock and simmer for 20 minutes, or until tender but always crisp. In a medium-size mixing dish, combine peas and remaining relish ingredients. Season with salt to taste and properly combine.

2. To smoke the tomatoes, firstly build and light a fire in a grill, preferably with hardwood charcoal briquettes. 6 to 8 aromatic wood chunks or 4 cups of wood chips can be soaked in warm water for 20 minutes.

3. After around 20 minutes, when the briquettes are glowing but mildly grey, apply the soaked wood chunks and let them flame for 5 minutes.

4. Tomatoes can be put on the grill. Cover the grill and smoke the tomatoes for 10 minutes before cutting them. Set aside the tomatoes after they have been peeled, seeded, and diced.

5. To sustain a hot fire with lots of red coals, add ample charcoal to the barbecue.

6. In a big skillet, melt the olive oil over medium-high heat to produce the smoked tomato sauce. Cook until the scallions, peppers, and serrano chilies are slightly tender around 3 minutes. Stir in the smoked tomatoes and cilantro, then season with salt and pepper to match. Takedown from the heat and put aside to stay warm.

7. To grill the snapper, spray either side with oil and cook for 4 minutes on either side on the barbecue or until opaque but always offering somewhat, not too soft or too rough. Add salt and freshly ground pepper as per the taste.

8. Divide the smoked tomato sauce equally among 4 warmed dinner plates to eat. Place a snapper fillet on top of the sauce and spoon-relish over it in a diagonal line. Serve right away.

11.5 GRILLED SNAPPER WITH CUMIN

Ready in about: 40 minutes - Servings: 4 - Difficulty: moderate

Ingredients:

- Vegetable oil.

- 4 (9-to 12-oz.) rose thorn snappers or 2 (1- to 2-lb.) Alaska red snappers or redfish, cleaned, heads on.

- ½ tsp. of cumin seeds.

- Kosher or coarse sea salt to taste.

- 4 tbsp. plus 2 tsp. of olive oil.

Instructions:

1. Clean the fish by rinsing it and patting it dry. Keep it refrigerated before you're able to use it.

2. In an outdoor grill, create and light a fire.

3. Preheat the oven to 300ª F.

4. When the coals are bright red and evenly dusted with dirt, use cooking oil and paper towels to properly oil the barbecue.

5. Cut 4 1/8-inch-deep holes through either side of each fish when the fire is blazing, using a very sharp knife blade to create cuts through the scales of the fish. Similar volumes of cumin seed (15 seeds is the optimum amount) should be tightly pressed into the cuts.

6. 2 tsp. of olive oil should be rubbed all over each trout. Place the fish on the grill such that the rungs are vertical under the fish's body. Cook for no more than 3 minutes per side for a small fish, 4 to 5 minutes for a big fish, or until golden grill marks appear.

7. Move fish to an oven-proof dish or baking sheet coated with foil with a finely oiled metal spatula and continue cooking in the oven until opaque within 8 to 10 minutes for a small fish, 15 to 20 minutes for a larger one. Stick the tip of a sharp knife through the meat just below the fish's head and pull out and see if it's cooked. It's best if the beef is translucent.

8. Place the remaining 4 tbsp. of olive oil in a flame-proof dish or ramekin and place it in the oven to heat gently around 5 minutes until the fish is done.

9. Place each fish in the middle of a dinner plate to eat. Pour 1 tbsp. of warm olive oil on 1 side of the fish and a thin strip of coarse salt on the other. Remove fillets from larger fish and put equal-sized pieces of fillet on each plate, seasoning with salt and oil. Serve right away.

11.6 GRILLED SARDINES

Ready in about: 30 minutes - Servings: 4 - Difficulty: moderate

Ingredients:

- 2 tbsp. of extra virgin olive oil.

- 24 medium or large sardines, cleaned.

- Salt and freshly ground pepper.

- Lemon wedges.

- A handful of sprigs of fresh rosemary.

Instructions:

1. Prepare a hot grill and make sure it's properly oiled. Sardines can be rinsed and dried with paper towels. Season with salt and pepper after tossing with olive oil.

2. Toss rosemary sprigs directly on the fire until the grill is primed. If required, wait for the flames to die down before placing sardines directly overheating in batches. Depending on distance, grill for 1 minute or 2 on either foot. Using tongs or a large metal spatula, move to a platter and serve with lemon wedges.

11.7   GINGER AND CHILI GRILLED SHRIMP

Ready in about: 1 hour and 15 minutes - Servings: 6 - Difficulty: moderate

Ingredients:

- 1 tbsp. of grated fresh ginger.
- 2 crushed cloves of garlic.
- ½ tsp. of freshly ground black pepper.
- ½ cup of low-fat buttermilk.
- 2 minced jalapeños.
- 1 tsp. of Kosher salt.
- 18 jumbo shrimp peeled and deveined, tails left on.
- 1 small lime, cut into 6 wedges.
- 2 ripe mangos, peeled, seeded, and cut into 1-inch dice.

Instructions:

1. In a medium mixing dish, combine buttermilk, ginger, jalapeños, salt, garlic, and pepper. To mix the ingredients, whisk them together. Toss in the shrimp and coat properly with a wooden spoon. Refrigerate for 1 hour to marinate.

2. Soak 6 wooden skewers for 10 minutes in hot. Alternating shrimp and mango, thread 3 shrimp and 2 mango bits into each skewer.

3. In the grill, start a fire. Grill shrimp for 4 to 6 minutes on either side until invisible, until the flames have died down and the coals are glowing. A wedge of lime should be served with each skewer.

11.8   GRILLED CLAMS WITH FRIED GARLIC

Ready in about: 15 minutes - Servings: 4 - Difficulty: easy

Ingredients:

- 3/4 cup extra virgin olive oil, plus more to brush on clams.
- 24 littleneck well-scrubbed clams.
- Juice of 1 lemon.
- ½ tsp. of red pepper flakes.
- 8 thinly sliced garlic cloves.

Instructions:

1. Prepare a grill for high-heat guided grilling.

2. Brush all sides of the clams with olive oil. Arrange them on the grate, cover, and cook for 3 to 6 minutes, or until the shells pop open.

3. Fill a baking dish with lemon juice big enough to accommodate all of the clams in 1 layer. Using tongs, transfer the clams to the serving bowl, being careful not to spill their juices.

4. In a shallow skillet on the grill, heat ¾ cup olive oil. When the pan is heated, add the garlic and cook for 1 to 2 minutes, or until golden brown. Stir in the pepper flakes for 15 seconds. Pour it over the clams.

5. Place the clams in 4 large pots. In a baking bowl, whisk the juices for 1 minute before pouring over the clams.

11.9   GRILLED CLAMS WITH LEMON AND CAYENNE BUTTER

Ready in about: 35 minutes - Servings: 2 - Difficulty: easy

Ingredients:

- Large pinch of kosher salt, more to taste.

- 2 tsp. of fresh lemon juice, more to taste.

- 1 large clove of garlic, minced.

- 4 tbsp. of melted unsalted butter.

- A pinch of cayenne pepper.

- Chopped fresh chives for serving.

- 2 dozen littleneck clams, scrubbed.

Instructions:

1. Mash garlic and salt along with a mortar and pestle or a flat section of a knife on a cutting board before a paste emerges. Scrap the paste into a shallow mixing cup, then add the lemon juice, butter, and cayenne pepper.

2. Preheat the grill to high. Place clams in a single layer on the grill grate or a big baking tray. Cover the grill and roast the clams for 2 minutes. Open the grill and inspect the clams, removing those that have opened with tongs and placing them in a wide tub. When moving the clams, be vigilant not to spill their juices. Close the cover on the grill and check it every 30 seconds, extracting the clams as they open.

3. Toss the clam bowl gently with the lemon-cayenne butter. Garnish with chives and serve promptly.

11.10   GRILLED SHRIMP WITH OLD BAY AND AIOLI

Ready in about: 35 minutes - Servings: 4 - Difficulty: easy

Ingredients:

- 1 lb. shell-on shrimp.

- 1 ½ tsp. of Old Bay seasoning.

- ½ cup plus 1 tbsp. canola oil, plus more for the grill.

- 3 small garlic cloves, finely grated, divided.

- ¾ tsp. of kosher salt.

- 2 lemons, divided.

- 1 egg yolk.

Instructions:

1. Preheat the grill to medium-high. Grates can be lightly oiled. Snip down the back of each shrimp shell with kitchen shears. Keep the shells on while grilling, so they function as a defensive shield.

2. Place the shrimp in a medium mixing dish. Toss in 1 tbsp. oil, 1 ½ tsp. Old Bay, 2/3 of the garlic, and ¾ tsp. salt. Enable it 10 to 15 minutes to rest as you make the aioli.

3. In a medium mixing dish, whisk together the egg yolk and the remaining garlic. Then take 1 tsp. lemon zest and finely grate it onto the egg mixture Whisk in the remaining ½ cup oil in a steady stream until the mixture is dense and light yellow. Half of the lemon juice should be added at this stage. Season to taste with salt.

4. Grill the shrimp and 3 lemon halves for 1 to 2 minutes, or until the shells change their color to a golden brown and are crispy in certain places, and the cut sides of the lemons are charred.

5. On a serving platter, spread the aioli. Arrange the burnt lemons and shrimp on top. Season with a pinch of Old Bay.

11.11 GRILLED RED SNAPPER WITH GREEN BEANS AND LIME

Ready in about: 35 minutes - Servings: 4 - Difficulty: easy

Ingredients:

- 1 small shallot, thinly sliced into rings.

- 1 tbsp. plus a ½ tsp. of light brown sugar.

- 4 skin-on red snapper fillets.

- 5 tsp. of fish sauce.

- 3 tbsp. plus a ¼ cup of extra-virgin olive oil, divided; plus, more for the grill.

- 4 tbsp. of lime juice.

- Kosher salt and ground pepper as per taste.

- 8 oz. of trimmed green beans.

- 2 tbsp. of salted crushed, dry-roasted peanuts.

Instructions:

1. Preheat the grill to medium-high heat and gently oil the grill grate. In a small bowl, mix 1 tbsp. lime juice, shallot, and ½ tsp. brown sugar; season with pepper and salt. Then, set it aside.

2. Clean the fish with paper towels and season it with pepper and salt all over. On a rimmed baking dish, toss the green beans with 1 tbsp. oil and season with pepper and salt. Grill beans until charred and softened in patches, around 2 minutes, rotating frequently. Place on a serving platter. Pat dry the fish once again and rub 2 tbsp. of oil onto the fillets. Place skin side down on grate and cook, undisturbed, for 6 to 8 minutes, or until flesh is opaque. Slide a small spatula underneath the fillet and flip it over, being careful not to tear the skin. Grill for another minute. Place on a plate with the green beans, skin side up.

3. In a small bowl, whisk together the fish sauce, the remaining ¼ cup of oil, the remaining 3 tbsp. lime juice, and the remaining 1 tsp. brown sugar until the sugar is completely dissolved. Drizzle the sauce over the fish and beans, then sprinkle the shallot mixture on top. Enable at least 15 minutes and up to 2 hours to marinate. If you're going to do it for more than 30 minutes, cover it and cool it. Allow cooling at room temperature.

4. Just before eating, sprinkle with peanuts.

11.12 CEDAR PLANKED SALMON

Ready in about: 35 minutes - Servings: 6 - Difficulty: easy

Ingredients:

- ⅓ cup of vegetable oil.

- 1 tsp. of sesame oil.

- ¼ cup of chopped green onions.

- 3 (12 inches) untreated cedar planks.

- 1 ½ tbsp. of rice vinegar.

- ⅓ cup of soy sauce.

- 1 tbsp. of grated fresh ginger root.

- 2 (2 lb.) salmon fillets, skin removed.

- 1 tsp. of minced garlic.

Instructions:

1. Soak the cedar planks in warm water for at least 1 hour. If you have time, soak for a longer period of time.

2. Combine the vegetable oil, sesame oil, rice vinegar, soy sauce, ginger, green onions, and garlic in a shallow container. Turn the salmon fillets in the marinade to seal them. Cover and set aside for at least 15 minutes, or up to 1 hour, to marinate.

3. Preheat a medium-hot outdoor grill. Arrange the planks on top of the grate. When the boards start to smoke and crackle a bit, they're primed.

4. Remove the salmon fillets from the marinade and place them on the planks. Cover and roast for about 20 minutes on the barbecue. When you can flake the fish with a fork, it's over. When you take it off the grill, it will begin to cook.

11.13 GRILLED BRANZINO WITH PRESERVED LEMON GREMOLATA

Ready in about: 35 minutes - Servings: 2 - Difficulty: easy

Ingredients:

- 1 tbsp. of olive oil.
- ½ tsp. of pepper.
- A small handful of fresh herbs—thyme, rosemary, sage, or parsley.
- 1 whole branzino or sub other whole fish.
- 1 tsp. of sea salt.
- 1 lemon.

Preserved lemon gremolata:

- ¼ cup of chopped preserved lemons (rind and flesh).
- ½ cup of olive oil.
- Optional chili flakes.
- 1 cup of finely chopped parsley.
- 2 finely chopped garlic cloves.
- Cracked pepper.

Instructions:

1. When buying a whole fish, ensure it has been descaled and gutted.

2. Rinse it thoroughly, then pat it dry thoroughly.

3. Apply a generous amount of oil to the brush.

4. Inside and out, season with pepper and salt.

5. Cram the slices of lemon into the fish's cavity. Add new herbs like rosemary, sage, thyme, or parsley.

6. Cut 3 to 4 slits through either side of the thick end of the fish with a sharp knife.

7. Heat the grill to 400° F and oil the grates. Reduce the heat to one side if necessary.

8. Place the fish on a hot, oiled grill with the tail facing down. Grill the fish for around 5 minutes, wrapped, without moving it, or until grill marks emerge.

9. To turn the pancakes, use tongs and a small metal spatula. Cover and barbecue for another 4 to 5 minutes, or until crisp with clear grill marks and eyes fog.

10. Create the flavorful preserved lemon gremolata while the fish is grilling by combining all of the required ingredients in a mixing bowl and stirring well.

11. Place the fish on a plate and drizzle the gremolata over the top just before serving.

12. Serve with a green salad and everyday quinoa.

11.14   GRILLED SALMON TZATZIKI BOWL

Ready in about: 30 minutes - Servings: 2 - Difficulty: easy

Ingredients:

- Olive oil.

- 1 lemon, sliced.

- 8 to 10 oz. of salmon.

- Pepper and salt.

Optional additions of bowl

- Cooked rice or quinoa, arugula, or other greens.

- Grilled veggies like eggplant, tomatoes, zucchini, peppers.

Fresh veggies:

- Radishes, tomatoes, cucumber, sprouts.

Garnish:

- Lemon, olive oil, and fresh herbs.

Instructions:

1. Preheat the grill to medium or high temperature.

2. Cook 1 cup of rice or quinoa according to box instructions on the grill.

3. Season the salmon with pepper and salt after brushing it with olive oil. Set it aside.

4. Tzatziki sauce may be made from scratch or purchased.

5. Place the salmon, as well as some other vegetables of your choice, on the grill (brush with pepper, olive oil, and salt). Grill the salmon for 4 minutes on both sides. Grill the lemon until it has a pleasant grill label.

6. Assemble the 2 bowls until the salmon and vegetables are cooked.

7. Divide the quinoa into 2 bowls. Add a couple of greens on top. Add some fresh vegetables you need, drizzle with olive oil, then season with pepper and salt. Overtop, place the grilled salmon and vegetables. Squeeze the lemon over the bowl as a final flourish. Cover the salmon with a couple of large spoonsful of tzatziki sauce. Fresh herbs like dill may be sprinkled on top. Then, serve.

CHAPTER 12 - CONCLUSION

We'd have to cook with less heat and lose taste if we didn't have the grill's searing high heat. Caramelization happens as proteins and sugars experience a transformation as a consequence of a chemical reaction that allows food to caramel as it heats. This gives grilled meats and vegetables a delicious increase of scent and taste. Consider marshmallows, caramelized onions, and, of course, the beef. They all taste ten times better when grilled.

Grilled food is simple, yet exotic food and the go-to food of every generation in the present world. Either the eldest member of the community or the youngest, everyone craves the grilled food.

This book covered a wide variety of grilling recipes that you can try at home with ease and become a pro at grilling.

Grilled food has its own benefits. This method of cooking lets you cook the food on direct heat in less amount of time and thus preserve the vital nutrients of the food. It is a technique that is age-old and is being followed since the very origin of the fire.

In this book, simple recipes were covered and you can easily try them at home. So, keep grilling.

Thank you and good luck!

GRILL COOKBOOK

For Beginners

Will Stone

Printed in Great Britain
by Amazon

64241248R00090